Spiritual Reading for the
Contemplative Christian

Visit www.booksurge.com to order additional copies.

REV. ROBERT E. ALBRIGHT

SPIRITUAL READING FOR THE CONTEMPLATIVE CHRISTIAN
30 HOMILIES AND SERMONS

2009

Spiritual Reading for the
Contemplative Christian

CONTENTS

ACKNOWLEDGMENTS

First of all, to the genius and giftedness of Huub Oosterhuis (poet, preacher, pastor), pastor of the Studenten Ekklesia in Amsterdam, Holland. To the Dutch publishers of his texts and music: Gooi & Sticht in Kampen, Kok Agora in Kampen, and Amboboeken-Bilthoven. To the musical composers of his many poems: Bernard Huijbers (May he rest in peace.), Antoine Oomen, and Tom Lowenthal, who brought these texts to life for the singing assembly.

To the American publishers who helped bring these works to our continent: Oregon Catholic Press, Jabulani Music, and North American Liturgy Resources. To Tom Conry and Tony Barr, whose efforts at publishing these texts and music on American soil have been heroic. To the publishers of his six volumes in English: Herder and Herder (*Open Your Hearts, Prayers Poems and Songs, Fifty Psalms*); Seabury (*At Times I See*); and Paulist Press (*Your Word is Near, Times of Life*).

To the many talented poets and translators who made it possible for these Dutch texts to be available for use in English-language liturgies throughout America and the Anglophonic world: Forrest Ingram, Juup van Beek, David Smith, Redmond McGoldrick (May he rest in peace.), Tony Barr, Mary Marousek, Tom Conry, Bill Tamblyn, Jim Hansen, Tom Schap, Cleophas Costello (May she rest in peace.), and Bernard Nachbahr (May he rest in peace.).

INTRODUCTION

I offer this volume of homilies and sermons for contemplation. Do not read them quickly, but at a slow pace, with time in between thoughts and certainly in between each homily or sermon. When embarking on one of these works, one should have quiet and time to meditate, reflect, ponder, and think about the thoughts, issues, and questions raised. May these homilies and sermons be a worthy addition to your prayer life. You might even need to read some more than once.

Following almost each homily or sermon is a text from the poems of the preeminent Dutch poet, Huub Oosterhuis, which I believe helps one to go beyond reading into full contemplation. These poems are liturgical in nature and act as a response on the part of the readers to the thoughts expressed in the particular homily or sermon that it is attached to. I hope you will find these prayerful and thought provoking in their own right.

As you can tell from the acknowledgments in this volume, many Dutch composers of liturgical music have used these poems. Translations of them exist in many languages, facilitating their use in many countries throughout the world. Here in the United States, I have had the privilege to work with these texts and music in numerous liturgical settings: Sunday and holy day liturgies, baptisms, weddings, funerals, in parishes, campus ministries, and small liturgical gatherings, as well as among Catholics, Protestants, Jews, and Muslims.

These and other texts of Oosterhuis have been an inspiration for many of my homilies and sermons over the years. I have been involved with these texts for the majority of my preaching ministry, as you can tell by reading any of my published volumes.

Keeping in mind the title of this volume, may the time you spend reading and contemplating be a time of prayer, challenge, education, and inspiration.

Father Bob Albright
March 2009

1.
MYSTERY OF THE TRINITY

Readings: Deuteronomy 4:32-34, 39-40 Romans 8:14-17
Matthew 28:16-20

If we go back to the beginning of the world for a moment, back to the time of primitive people, the Stone Age, the Iron Age, the Bronze Age (to people like Grog or the Flintstones), or to more serious and real people like the Egyptians, Abraham, and Moses, we can picture these people struggling with the forces of nature in order to keep alive. Nature was their salvation and sometimes their destruction. In those days, men and women were preoccupied with the forces in nature and it was in these forces that they discovered God: voice from the fire, cloud in the distance, the roar of mighty waters, thunder, and the sun. Nature was precious to these people and they took their most precious treasures from nature to form their gods of gold and silver. They were not so sure who or what kind of god operated these forces in nature, so they formed statues of animals, or half-human half-animal, or even monster-like creatures. People saw the treasures of nature not only as necessary to possess god in this life, but also, as with the Pharaohs in Egypt, a necessary item to be buried with for the afterlife.

As people developed and slowly conquered nature, they had more time to become human, to develop socially and intellectually. They became more and more aware of themselves as persons, as creatures of God. And, when the time was right, a son came to reveal God to us in the person of Jesus. In the man Jesus it has become known that God is not only in the forces of nature, but also that God is human. In this person, the Gospels tell us, we can come to know who God is. In these Gospels, we find a man to whom life is precious, people are precious, and the service of his brothers and sisters is all he possesses. He possesses no money, no wealth, no gold or silver. He possesses only life and is willing to give even that up for the service of others. He worships no idols or statues, nor partakes of any sacrifices to the gods. He does only the will of one God he calls "Abba," "Father." He drinks the cup of human sorrow. He endures the blows of rejection and hate. He even goes to his death. In him, we have discovered a God who is not far away but is a part of people.

Today, science has conquered much of the myth caused by the forces of nature and the problems that ancient people experienced. Today, Jesus Christ, the Son of God, no longer walks the earth making God physically present in our midst. Today people ask: "Where is your God? Let him rise up. Let him appear before us. We want to see him. What good to us is just a name?" Today, we do not know where to look for God. Some still look at statues and tabernacles made of gold. Some still look at the beauty and might of nature. Some still look to the stars and planets. Some still look to laws and rituals. And like the Stone Age person, we find no response, no answer to our questions, no recognition that we exist, no promises fulfilled, no one.

But rather, we should come of age and know that God is present in spirit, the same spirit who breathed life into people in the beginning, the same spirit that animated Jesus with power, the same spirit that lives in each of us whether we believe or not. When we live as Jesus lived, his spirit lives in us. When life becomes precious to us, when people come alive because of us, God lives in us. When we respond to another in need, we become a hand that sets free and give others hope that there is a God. When we recognize someone who is never noticed, that someone might find God in us. When there is love between friends, between spouses or partners, between man and woman, woman and woman, man and man, between enemies, there is God. When we are willing to forgive those who hurt us, we become God for another. There seems to be nowhere else to go, but to one another, to find God.

The mystery of trinity—one God—three persons—Father, Son, and Holy Spirit. What meaning does "trinity" have in your life? Is it just some insolvable mystery contrived by some religious Sherlock Holmes? Or is it a mathematical game of three in one? Or is it a dogma divorced from life, impossible to be understood, concealed and blinding? Or is it real? Is it a lived experience?

The mystery of trinity is the mystery of life itself—eternal—a depth that is unfathomable—sometimes clear, sometimes confusing, never being able to fill the needs of all—never being able to be filled yourself. The trinity is not only to be contemplated, but also lived. The mystery then is life itself—how to live together—how to be in each other—how to see all people as our equals. We cannot separate the mystery of the trinity from the mystery of life. For to live **is** God. And it is in **doing** God that we find God. And we must find God in ourselves before we can see God in others.

Trinity—God—life. Contemplating the trinity and living life are one and the same mystery!

HE SAYS HE IS GOD

He says he is God
let him appear before us.
What good to us is just a name?
Let him rise up—we want to see him.
Voice from the fire, cloud in the distance
are not enough
for this earth of splinters and smoke
where we are granted no life.

Words and miracles are in abundance
and gods of gold, of gold and promises,
but not a god—like a hand that sets free,
someone who does what he says.

You who say that you are our God,
concealed and blinding, impossible you,
what keeps you away from people?
Can you endure the blows
that people endure?

REV. ROBERT E. ALBRIGHT

Can you drink the cup
that we have to drink?
Will you go with us to death?

2.
TRINITY AS COMMUNITY

Readings: Proverbs 8:22-31 Romans 5:1-5 John 16:12-15

Trinity is a mystery and revelation of God unique only to Christianity!

If I or anyone would ask you—What is the Christian concept or belief about God?—Your answer would be **Trinitarian**! The Christian believes in the Trinitarian concept of God!

The trinity is a logical conclusion to all the revelation afforded us in the New Testament (the Christian Scriptures).

As followers of Jesus, the Christ, we are believers in the three *faces* of God, of the three *personas* revealed and named as "the Father," "the Son," and "the Holy Spirit."

One God—three persons—three persons in one God.

The early Church fathers grappled with this revelation and defined it in a most unique way, leaving it as a mystery, not only to be contemplated, but also to be lived.

The mystery of the trinity is the basis for all of Christianity since it alone holds the three major revealed mysteries of our Scripture: that God is the transcendent creator of all things; that God is the Lord of history, becoming human and offering the world salvation; that God is all pervasive and imminent, always with us, as a source of grace aiding us humans to live in a relationship with the divine.

The early Church fathers named these three mysteries as Creation—Salvation—Sanctification (Life—Love—Grace).

Traditionally, we have spoken these mysteries within the basic mystery of the trinity by calling God the Father "creator," God the Son "savior," and God the Holy Spirit "sanctifier."

Yet we know and believe that God is the one and only God. The oneness of God is the unity in the Godhead, the community of the Godhead—three persons equal in divine nature—not three parts of divinity—not three pieces of the pie—not three gods—but three persons in one God!

In other words, God is ultimately **community**!

St. Thomas Aquinas used the image of the mirror to teach the reality of how three can be one: *Self* (the first entity) looks into a mirror and sees a *reflection* (the second entity) and experiences a *relationship* (the third entity) between the *self* and the *reflection*.

St. Patrick used the symbol of the shamrock to teach the concept of the trinity: three leaves in one plant.

Father Felix Malmberg, SJ, theology professor at Loyola College in Baltimore, using the symbol of eternity (the horizontal numeral eight) would take his finger and trace the symbol in midair while describing the trinity as "being in each other." And he would say to his students: "If you ask the Father, 'Who are you?' He would say, 'I am the Son and the Holy Spirit.' If you ask the Son, 'Who are you?' He would say, 'I am the Father and the Holy Spirit.' If you ask the Holy Spirit, 'Who are you?' She would say, 'I am the Father and the Son.'"

The mystery of the trinity, then, is the mystery of perfect **community**, of how to live together, how to be in each other, how to allow the other to help define one's own identity, how to see all people as our equals, how to live life for everyone!

The mystery of the trinity cannot be separated from the mystery of life, the mystery of love, the mystery of grace. God **is** Life! God **is** Love! God **is** Grace! And God is one!

If we live life to our fullest capacity, then we are **doing** God. If we love till it kills us, then we are **doing** God. If we give life to others, then we are **doing** God. For it is in **doing** God that we find God. And we discover not some pie-in-the-sky god, but the real God, living here among us, always creating us anew, always saving us from our limitations, always giving us another chance to become human.

Community, then, is a valid experience of God—perhaps even the most valid. We most strongly experience and best express the mystery of the trinity by living in **community**.

The dogma of the trinity, then, says that **God is community**, and that humans have been created in the image and likeness of God—that is—**COMMUNITY!**

3.
GOD AS FATHER

God is never called nor referred to as "father" in the entire Torah. The earliest reference to God as father in the whole Old Testament dates from after the Babylonian exile, and shows up only twice in the prophetic books and twice in the wisdom literature.

Apparently, what's *new* in the New Testament is the ease with which its authors call God, "father." Edward Schillebeeckx, in his book, *Jesus*, makes the claim that "abba" is probably the only word in the New Testament that we can be somewhat sure Jesus actually spoke. Therefore, it becomes obvious why the Evangelists and Paul use the title so often.

Abba, of course, is the Aramaic rendition of "father," which literally means, even today in Hebrew, "daddy." Jesus called God, "daddy"—an intimate title for an intimate relationship.

Since the Gospel of Matthew is the most Jewish of all four Gospels and uses the term "father" quite often, let's use this Gospel to examine this image more closely.

Right from the beginning of Matthew's Gospel, he exposes his readers to the image of "father." His genealogy of Jesus suggests that Jesus is the product of a whole history of exemplar human fathers who were carrying out God's plan by the way they lived their lives—thus Abraham was the father of Isaac; Isaac, the father of Jacob; and Jacob, the father of Judah and his brothers. All these fathers of Israel's history were able to carry out God's plan, because they knew God's plan, because they knew God in an intimate, face-to-face relationship. (Cf. Matthew 1:1-17.)

The final father in this entire history is Joseph, who becomes the earthly or legal father of Jesus. Of Joseph, Matthew says, he was upright and obedient to the Law. And just like the fathers in Israel's history, Joseph too obeys the will of God dictated to him in dreams, and thus becomes an instrument of God's plan. (Cf. Matthew 1:18-25.)

Personally, through Joseph, and communally, through all the fathers of Israel, Jesus experiences the positive and life-giving effects of true fatherhood. There can be no greater motive than this as to why in his adult life Jesus turns to calling God his father. His experience of "father" was a good one. His experience of "God" was a good one. He put them together for his followers by calling God "Father." He even taught his followers to pray by saying, "Our Father." (Cf. Matthew 6:9.)

Throughout his Gospel, Matthew cites thirty-three times when Jesus uses the image of "father" in reference to God and directly calls God "Father." In Matthew's Gospel, then, God, the Father, becomes the model for all human fatherhood.

"Be perfect as your heavenly Father is perfect" (5:48).

In Matthew's Gospel, a father cares for, provides for, and nurtures his children.

"Look at the birds in the sky. They do not sow or reap, they gather nothing into barns—yet your heavenly Father feeds them. Are not you more important than they" (6:26)?

In Matthew's Gospel, a father is a faithful steward who acts with integrity.

"Which one of you would hand his child a stone when she asks for a loaf of bread, or a snake when he asks for a fish? If you then, who are wicked, learn how to give good gifts to your children, how much more will your heavenly Father give good things to those who ask him" (7:9-11)?

In Matthew's Gospel, a father is centered in his vocation, stable in his emotions, thoughtful in his actions, generous, kind, and calm.

"Amen I say to you, if two of you agree on earth about anything for which they are to pray, it shall be granted to them by my heavenly Father" (18:19).

In Matthew's Gospel, a father is passionate, alive, playful, and sensual—sensitive in his relations with his children, boundless, and mystical.

"I give praise to you, Father, Lord of heaven and earth, for although you have hidden things from the wise and the learned you have revealed them to the childlike. Yes, Father, such has been your gracious will. All things have been handed over to me by my Father. No one knows the Son except the Father, and no one knows the Father except the Son—and anyone to whom the Son wishes to reveal him" (11:25-27).

In Matthew's Gospel, a father passes on blessing and order to his children. He makes laws and sets boundaries. In his wisdom, he teaches his children by word and example.

"Where did this man get such wisdom and mighty deeds? Is he not the carpenter's son? Is not his mother named Mary and his brothers James, Joseph, Simon, and Judas? Are not his sisters all with us? Where did this man get all this" (13:54-56)?

In Matthew's Gospel, a father must be a reconciler, a transformer, a counselor, and able to discern the truth for his children.

"The master summoned the servant and said to him, 'You wicked servant! I forgave you your entire debt because you begged me to. Should you not have had pity on your fellow servant, as I had on you?' Then in anger his master handed him over to the torturers until he should pay back the whole debt. So will my heavenly Father do to you, unless each of you forgives your brother and sister from your heart" (18:32-35).

In Matthew's Gospel, a father has to be ascetic, disciplined, courageous, aggressive, and able to defend valid boundaries.

"My Father, if it is possible, let this cup pass me by; yet not my will, but yours be done" (26:39).

"Do you think that I cannot call upon my Father and he will provide me at this moment with more than twelve legions of angels? But then how would the Scriptures be fulfilled which say that it must come to pass in this way" (26:53-54)?

In Matthew's Gospel, a father is someone who does everything in his power to rescue his child from harm and death.

"And behold, the angel of the Lord appeared to (his father) Joseph in a dream and said, 'Rise, take the child and his mother, flee to Egypt and stay there until I tell you. Herod is going to search for the child to destroy him!' Joseph rose and took the child and his mother by night and departed for Egypt. He stayed there until the death of Herod, that what the Lord had said through the prophet might be fulfilled, OUT OF EGYPT I CALLED MY SON" (2:13-15).

And so, as you continue to reflect on this image, let your prayer rise up in the words of this song:

SONG TO LIGHT

Bright morning light that breaks upon us,
first early light in which we are
alone and cold and so uncertain;
oh light, surround me, urge me on.
I would not stray from you;
and let us not, helpless, aimless as we are,
stray far away from one another
and fall into the endless night.

Wise light, the steward of my city,
the faithful light that overcomes;
dear father light with strong firm shoulders
then lift me up I am your child.
Look thru my eyes child in me, pure light,
and see if somewhere worlds exist
where people live a life of goodness,
where people bear their names in peace.

All things will yield and give away all
that is not rooted in the light.
Our words will only sow destruction,
nothing remains of what we do.
But light, your own clear voice is singing
in every heart that lives on earth.
All people love you, light, the first born,
oh light, last word of one who lives.

4.
THE GOD OF SINAI

Readings: Isaiah 40:1-5, 9-11 Psalm 24 II Peter 3:8-14 Mark 1:1-8

If you can remember—back when we were kids—you might have been asked the question, "Where is God?" And we were taught to answer, "God is everywhere!"

In the prophecy from Isaiah, primitive Israel finds the answer to this question on a mountain. Contrary to our catechisms of old, the God of people is a God of the mountain—God most high. The mountains came forth from the hand of God, who made them as a witness to God's power, and it is there that God dwells.

The God in this prophecy is "up there"—removed, isolated, above it all, not a part of people, watching over them, checking on them, silent, on top of everything! God is unseen, unreachable, not to be grasped. God is there only to impart laws and receive worship.

For Israel, it is *on* a mountain that God first appears. It is *on* a mountain that God lives and reigns. It is *from* the mountain that God gives the old and new covenants. It is *on* a mountain that God dies. It is *in* a mountain that he is buried. It is *from* the mountain that he takes leave of his people, and we are left with the question, "Why are you standing here looking into the sky" (Acts 1:11)?

We search for God. Where is God? God is not "up there" enthroned on high, no rock, no firm foundation, no neat round number or standard rule, no doomsday hanging over us, far away, yet near, not here, not everywhere, not that kind of a God we keep dreaming.

In our own lives, we are people who have our ups and downs, our frustrations and peak experiences. We live a life full of love and hatred, experiencing ecstasy and misery, and boring and delighting others and ourselves. We despair at the thought of leaving the foot of the mountain. We find it harder to reach out than to climb up. Who, then, can climb to the height of God? People—who realize that reaching God is reaching other people—people—who do not build their lives on appearances—people—who do not forge lies against others—people—who are willing to take a risk!

In the 1960s, the Rev. Martin Luther King Jr. walked the nation. He had seen people persecuted. He had seen injustice. He had seen a world of hate and prejudice. And dreaming of a future when men and women would live together in peace and contemplating a world fit to live in, he said, "I have a dream. I have been to the mountain." The God of the mountain is the God of people—struggling with them in their dreams and hopes for a better earth—a God who is willing to die so that we are free to live. God's life must again and again be like that of the man from Nazareth who was killed for no reason by other people.

To some degree we are all guilty of remaining at the foot of the mountain—content to seek a God "up there"—content to be the receiver of some law or word which will make our life more secure—content to receive an answer. There are no answers! There are only people—you and me—women and men—this person or that person. The answer to the question, "Where is God?" will not be found "up there" on the mountain, but rather right here, all around us. Look around!

I suppose God is right here among us or everywhere. If God exists somewhere, then God is all—the living, the dying, refugee, stranger. God is people. God is human. God is the least among people. God is Jesus of Nazareth who tells us, "The hour is coming when you will worship the Father neither on this mountain nor in Jerusalem, but you shall worship him in spirit and truth." (Cf. John 4:21-23.)

Maybe then we can grasp Isaiah's hope and vision for Israel (and we are Israel): "Make straight in the wasteland a highway for our God! Every valley shall be filled in, every mountain and hill shall be made low; the rugged land shall be made a plain, the rough country a broad valley. Then the glory of the Lord shall be revealed, and all humankind shall see it together...Go up onto a high mountain...and cry out without fear: Here is your God!"

SONG AT THE FOOT OF THE MOUNTAIN

You, naming you is all in vain
no road can reach your far domain
nor any word adore you.
You, not up there enthroned on high
but light that dims in cloudy sky
or tale of vanished glory.
You come, we know not day nor hour
you pass nearby, a breath of fire
a stillness through trees streaming
crying far off yet near us, too
not here or everywhere are you
not that god we keep dreaming.

No nice safe path to walk along
no spot or leg to stand upon
no rock, no firm foundation.
No heart that speaks, no spurting springs
no blood that wells and swells and sings
no soul for contemplation.
No neat round number, standard rule
no doomsday hanging over all
in dire and dreadful fashion.
But you are people maimed and small
the homeless nameless people—all
who cry out for compassion.

Resounding stillness, voice so thin
if you exist, exist in them
in people all around us.
If you are not and cannot be,

elusive word, come be in me
no god we make an idol.
You know me and you bind me tight
I cry out "you" both day and night
and cannot quite forget you;
how then could we be I alone
be homeless nameless and forlorn
and how not know each other?

5.
CORPUS CHRISTI

Readings: Deuteronomy 8:2-3, 14b-16a I Corinthians 10:16-17
John 6:51-58

As any farmer knows, or even any one of us who has studied biology or worked with plants, for a seed to have any effect it must die, go underground into the darkness, be buried and trampled underfoot. It must be scattered, hidden, lost, unnoticed, ignored, drenched in the rain, and scorched by the sun.

Then the seed lives, it rises, it is reborn, it comes to life, it sprouts, it pushes through the hard ground, it blossoms, it revives, it springs into existence unnoticed, it grows, it changes, it matures, it becomes beautiful, it flowers, it produces fruit, it responds to the light of the sun.

Taken even further, the seed becomes the wheat for bread and the grapes for wine. It must undergo more change as it is baked into bread or crushed to make wine. As bread and wine it still undergoes change, because people break the bread and chew it up, they pour the wine and drink it down. The tiny seed goes on living and nourishing people. Then people become seed, who must also die in order to live, who must also be buried in order to rise, who must also be hidden in order to bear fruit. A person becomes the grain of wheat, the grape, in order to become another's bread and wine. Like the smallest seed, we are destined to feed each other.

People must live, then, for others. This is life. In the Gospel, Jesus makes this clear when he says, "The person who wishes to save his life must first lose it." Jesus makes this even clearer by his own life. He gave himself totally to people. He lived life to the full. He loved without limit. He offered himself as seed, as the beginning, as the first among people, as the example of how all life must be—giving one's body and life's blood to others.

When we go to communion, then, we are communicating with a person who went the way of all seed and is now our bread, a person who was poured out and emptied himself and is now our wine, a person who lived and died for others and still lives for us. He is the seed—the beginning. He is the resurrection and the life—the end. He is bread and wine—Eucharist. He is human—God!

And so, my friends, what I speak of is a mystery, and every time you go to communion you step into this mystery once again. It will take you the rest of your life (and perhaps even more) to fathom it. No one expects you to know and experience its fullness in this life. No one of us is capable of telling you everything about it. That's what a mystery is—something we go on and on with, always discovering something new about it, growing with it, learning from it, never quite putting our finger on it, yet drawing strength from it, becoming and being more and more who we are because of it.

This mystery is both wonderful and terrible. It will both satisfy and demand. It is the mystery of Jesus in whom God and people are united. It is our own mystery, for Jesus is human. It is the mystery of the seed. We call it "Eucharist." This is wonderful and seems satisfying that we should partake of such a great mystery. Yet, it is a mystery that demands giving and sharing, risk and commitment, dying and rising. Remember—for the seed to flourish, it first had to undergo the hardship of being buried and trampled upon. For this reason, whenever you receive communion, it will not be bread in its wholeness, but broken bread, passed from hand to hand, shared, and eaten up. Jesus lived this mystery too and he calls every one of his followers to do the same. When we are willing to live out this mystery in our own lives, then we are in communion with the one who lived it to perfection.

This is communion—when you too are willing to become more and more like him whom you eat; when you too are willing to be broken and shared, passed from hand to hand, eaten up, when you too are willing to be bread for others whatever the cost; when you too are willing to love without limit. This is not easy to do. It will become clearer to you now that the life of a Christian is not an easy one. And it is in going to communion when we recognize this most.

So, my friend, when you go to communion again and again for the rest of your life, know this—that it is your own mystery you are receiving. It is your own life that you hold in your hands. As you eat of this mystery over and over again, as you break bread over and over, as you drink from the cup again and again, may you come to know who you are, and may you find God in the life you give to others.

SONG OF ALL SEED

Whoever wants to live like God on earth,
must go the way all seed must go,
and so will find rebirth.

You go the way of every earthly thing.
With heart and soul you live the lot
of every death-bound being.

To sun you're handed over and to rain.
The tiny seed in wind and storm
must die to live again.

Yes, we must learn to die for one another.
The tiny seed becomes the bread
that people feed each other.

So God becomes that seed and finds rebirth.
In death, our God gave life and bread
to everyone on earth.

6.
THE BODY AND BLOOD OF JESUS

Readings: Exodus 24:3-8 Hebrews 9:11-15 Mark 14:12-16, 22-26

In the Bible, the concept of *body* is a symbol of the self, of me, of I, of the person. When Jesus said, "Take this bread and eat it, this is my body," he was really saying, "This bread is me, my very self, eat of me!"

In the Bible, the concept of *blood* is a symbol of life, of animation, of that which was the force that made the body move, of the force itself, which came from God and was that part of God we humans shared. In the Bible, blood=life! Read Leviticus 17:10-14.

Life's blood…life:
in English, Blood
in Hebrew, (Dam)
in Greek, (Aima)
in Latin, Sanguis
in Polish, Krew
in French, Le Sang
in German, Das Blut
in Dutch, Bloed
in Italian, Sangue
in Russian, KpoB
in Spanish, Sangre
in Chinese, (Sooay)

Because blood was understood as life itself, Moses, in the Book of Exodus, sprinkles both the altar (symbolizing God) and the people (Israel) with the blood of the animal as a liturgical expression of the union between God and Israel in the living covenant. God gave a new life to Israel through the Torah, the covenant. Similarly, the Church sprinkles water (another symbol of life) on its people to remind us of our covenant in baptism. God gives a new life to Gentiles through the blood of Jesus.

Because blood was understood as life itself, the author of the Letter to the Hebrews can make the analogy of atonement from the blood of the lamb in the Old Testament to the blood of Christ in the New Testament—the same covenant symbolized for Jews by the lamb's blood and symbolized for Christians by Christ's blood. In both Testaments, blood is the symbol of our atonement for sin. Blood, then, is not only life for the body, but for the spirit, as well.

At the Last Supper found in Mark's Gospel comes the union of *body* and *blood*, already symbols of self and life, now being liturgically expressed in symbols of bread and wine. Using the Biblical Hebrew understanding of *body* and *blood*, Jesus says, this is me, this is life. "This is my body"—Jesus is bread—Jesus gives himself! "This is my blood"— Jesus is wine—Jesus gives life!

Bread is the grain of the field. Wine is the fruit of the vine.

Then Jesus says, "Truly I tell you, I will never again drink of the fruit of the vine until that day when I drink it new in the Kingdom of God" (Mark 14:25).

Drinking a cup of wine is symbolic of participating in life, of being alive. Jesus is indicating his own life on this earth is over and a new life awaits him in the Kingdom of God.

In the Gospel of John, at the moment of his death, Jesus cries out, "I am thirsty." He is given sour wine to drink and then dies. It is as if this is no longer the life he has to live, it has gone sour, it is finished. Then he is pierced with a lance upon which blood and water come out. Blood and water—both symbols of life—both symbols of atonement. Jesus' death was both an atonement and life giving.

And so we Christians express this saving mystery in our own liturgies by sprinkling water, breaking bread, and drinking wine.

Wine—the fruit of the vine—the nectar of life. Wine—the seed, the vine, the grape, the fruit, the juice—a process of the seed dying and rising, of darkness into light, of growth, of blooming, of being picked, of being crushed, of changing, of fermenting, of aging.

Wine:
in Hebrew, (Ya'Yeen)
in Greek, (Krassi)
in Latin, Vinum
in Polish, Wino
in French, Le Vin
in German, Der Wein
in Dutch, Wijn
in Spanish and Italian, Vino
in Russian, (Vihno)
in Chinese, (Putaojiu)

in every language, LIFE!

(*Foreign words in parentheses are phonetic renditions and not the actual alphabet.*)

IN THE MIDST OF DEATH

People live this life in the midst of dying,
one who broke the bread also lives as people
in the midst of death.

Death is in our blood, death before our seeing
but he gives us hope, so we go on living
death within our blood.

That we rise from death, so to go on living
we must eat the bread he for us has given
in the midst of death.

Death before our eyes, death within our being
give us weary ones lamp to guide our stumbling
light for us to see.

Be for us our bread, Jesus who is risen
that we live in you life as it is given
in the midst of death.

Be the wine we drink, cup to quench the living
be the pain we feel, be for us a refuge
as we live in you.

7.
EUCHARIST AS MYSTERY

E ucharist is the mystery of…

GIVING AND RECEIVING
Eucharistia (Greek) = thanksgiving gift.

We have been given a new life in Jesus.

We celebrate that new life by returning our worship and faith.

We call this thanksgiving the Mass or Eucharist(ia).

Eucharist is the mystery of…

REDEMPTION
Of what God has given to us through Jesus.

Of the forgiveness of our sins.

Note the words in the Last Supper "my blood, shed for the forgiveness of your sins."

In receiving Eucharist, we receive forgiveness.

We do not stay away from this sacrament because we are unworthy. It is precisely *because* we are unworthy that we need it most!

The Eucharist is redemption and redemption is forgiveness.

Eucharist is the mystery of…

COVENANT
Of our response to God's redemption…

How we live—why we live—the way we live.

That is where we worship God—in our everyday lives.

The Mass or liturgy is not worship—it is where we express our worship, where we express our everyday lives.

Eucharist is the mystery of…

BREAD AND WINE
Bread: *Seed*, planted and trampled underfoot in darkness, scorched by the sun and drenched in the rain. Then it blossoms and becomes

wheat! *Wheat*, kneaded into dough and baked. Then it becomes bread! *Bread*, broken and chewed up. Then it becomes the *body of people*!

Wine: *Seed*, planted and trampled underfoot in darkness, scorched by the sun and drenched in the rain. Then it blossoms and becomes grapes! *Grapes*, crushed and mutilated. Then it becomes wine! *Wine*, poured out and drunk or swallowed. Then it becomes the *blood of people*!

Eucharist is the mystery of…

BODY AND BLOOD

Of being eaten up, being used, passed from hand to hand, broken, emptied like a cup, shared out, given away.

In Hebrew, body = self, total self—the outward manifestation of who we are—self.

In Hebrew, blood = life.

When Jesus spoke those words saying, "This is my body…this is my blood," he was really saying, "This is me—this is my life given for you."

Eucharist is the mystery of…

SELF

Himself and yourself.

You become what you eat and drink.

You become yourself.

You become his body.

Ezekiel was told to eat the scroll (the word of God) and became a prophet.

St. Augustine said when you come to communion with your hands outstretched,

you hold your own mystery in your hands.

Eucharist is the mystery of…

REMEMBERING

Who he was and who we are.

Zikkar (Hebrew) = To make the past present.

To re-member is the opposite of dis-member.

To put Jesus back together again, but into ourselves (our minds and bodies)!

Anamnesis (Greek) = to remember!

SPIRITUAL READING FOR THE CONTEMPLATIVE CHRISTIAN

Eucharist is the mystery of…

THE MEAL

Of table fellowship, of community, of communion.

When we eat with people, we are most vulnerable. We are defenseless and open. We carry no weapons. We experience friendship and cordiality. Strangers who come to church and go to communion become friends. The self is exposed.

The meal = the image of the Kingdom of God (the Eternal Banquet).

Jesus' appearances after the resurrection were mostly at meals such as Emmaus, the upper room where the Last Supper was held, around a campfire, etc.

Many parables of Jesus centered on meals and food.

Heavy concepts like heaven, salvation, and eternal life are all imaged in the Scripture as meals, where food and drink will be flowing in abundance.

Eucharist is the mystery of…

PRESENCE AND ABSENCE

When someone is no longer with us in one way, we discover new ways of experiencing their presence—memory, story, pictures, images, comparisons, etc.

For the early Church—the Jesus from Nazareth who walked among them and became absent through death on a cross was present in a different way in the risen Christ, whom they then called JESUS CHRIST!

Physical presence is sometimes an obstacle to intimate communication (e.g., a friend or relative visiting—joy sometimes turns to dislike when we are faced with their physical idiosyncrasies). In absence, from a distance, we see each other in a new way. We are less distracted by each other's idiosyncrasies and are better able to see and understand each other's inner core.

Eucharist is the inner core of Jesus the Christ!

Eucharist is the mystery of…

SACRAMENT

The moment, the place, the gesture where God and people meet!

Jesus *met* God in death. Jesus was *called* God in death. Jesus was *raised* by God from death!

Therefore, for us, the death and resurrection of Jesus becomes a sacrament—the moment, the gesture, the place where we too can meet God—where we too die to self, take up **our** cross and rise to a new life.

The Eucharist, then, is too complicated a mystery and too large a scope to be experienced only once like many other sacraments. Therefore, the Church celebrates it over and over, again and again, hoping that someday we're all going to get it right!

HUNCH

Now I have you in my head
like a whirlwind,
a wild flood of notions.
Now like a bull's eye,
a shot in my heart,
an aweful, terrible
hunch in my bones.

Full of your presence and full of your absence,
I wait
all my life long, if I must
and I do not care who knows it.

8.
THE BODY OF CHRIST

When we Christians gather, we gather as a body. As individuals, certainly, but individuals who make up (together) what St. Paul calls the body of Christ. As individuals, we sin. But the individual sinner does not work toward reconciliation alone. The sinner is reconciled to God through the mediation of the Church, which in itself is the sacrament of reconciliation. For we, the Church, have been won through the blood of Christ shed on the cross. For it was on the cross that the Church was born. It is the entire Church that prays, sustains, and asks pardon. An individual, is not only associated with others in sin, but also associated with others in a return to God. This means that the whole of the Christian community must be striving toward renewal.

When we gather together in a church—we are not each going our own ways—but rather are going each other's way by coming together. This is a sign—this is the Church—this is the only way it can be done! One man or one woman cannot go it alone! Together we can move mountains—mountains of guilt and sins—mountains of greed and prejudice. Together we can build cities—cities of peace and love. And *as* we do this and *because* we do this, we become his body! Certainly not as perfect as that body should be—but because we come together, there is hope for that, for a future, for striving, for a kingdom of peace, justice, and love.

In the Gospel, this kingdom is likened to a banquet, to a grain of wheat, to paradise, to the vineyard, to the forgiving and merciful father, to those who live their lives for others. Jesus is the image and likeness of this kingdom—for the Gospel calls him bread for the life of the world and knows that he expressed the mystery of his life in a meaningful gesture—that he broke bread and gave it to be eaten and thus to become a new person. The Church—we—his body—must be born again and again from the Gospel. We must recognize in that gesture of Jesus of Nazareth the mystery of life itself—for no one lives for himself and no one dies for herself. We go to church to join in a banquet of love—we break and share the bread—this little defenseless gesture, which is always the same, is a gesture toward him. It means we want to remember him, keep him in mind, imitate him in our lives, go out to meet him in hope, that we see our salvation in the man he was and in the God he called his Father. It means that we believe in giving and receiving, in belonging together, in the mystery of our own lives.

————This banquet and the gesture of breaking bread is also a desperate gesture in which we admit that we cannot quite complete it and that we do not know how to do it on a worldwide scale. It is an impotent gesture against world hunger and an expression of our collective guilt. We use an image and sense that it is still not a reality—for many people are still starving in our world—not just for bread, but also for peace. At this moment men, women, and children are suffering from starvation. At this moment there is unrest and killing in the world. But also at this moment you and I gather to give of ourselves—to express this in money and food for the poor, a part of ourselves, and also in that simple gesture of feeding each other. And in these expressions we hold to that vision of a future world where there is justice, where everyone has his and her fill, where we do not tear each other to pieces, but **do** what is unthinkable and impossible and **are** what we cannot yet be—people living in peace!

NO ONE

No one lives for himself.
No one dies for herself.
We live and we die for God alone.
To God alone we belong.

9.
ECCLESIA

Readings: Ezekiel 47:1-2, 8-9, 12 Psalm 46 I Corinthians 3:9-17 John 2:13-22

The New Jerusalem—the holy city—spotless bride—dwelling place of God—new heaven—new earth—God's building—temple of God—temple of living stones—house of prayer—body of Christ—people.

What prophet or poet would be courageous enough to improve on these names and images given to the Church?

The Church—what is it? Or better yet, who is it? St. Paul says that it is the "mystery which has been hidden since the beginning of the world" (Col. 1:24-29). In the Old Testament, God began to plan for the life of the Church. Like all living bodies, the Church experienced a stage of pregnancy. Like the fetus or unborn child, it grew in the womb of humanity, slowly working its way from darkness into the light. Hidden in the womb of many ages, not visible, concealed, not free to move on its own, the Church was felt within the community of Israel. They dreamt about it. They speculated about its birth and life. They gave it many names. They had visions about its future. They touched it and felt it occasionally to see if it was still alive. They complained when it kicked from within and caused the pains of exile in a foreign land. Yet they rejoiced in its somewhat bewildering presence.

In the New Testament, the Church was born and revealed to all who would accept it. It was born in a child who became human in people. It was founded in and through Jesus of Nazareth. It became his body and took on the shape and character of all people—people who accepted Jesus and his way of life—people who wanted to carry out his work and keep his words alive—people who believed that Jesus still lived in their midst—people who would go on living and dying for each other as he did—children, men, and women in whom his spirit dwelt.

Since that time, and over the centuries, the Church has matured like you and me, a product of God and people. With the stamina of youth and the growing pains of childhood it has experienced sanctity and sin, conversions and heresies, inquisitions and liberation, triumph and persecutions, rejection and acceptance.

And what about now—at what stage of life is the Church today? A few years ago one of my students suggested that the Church is now going through adolescence—a period of turmoil and confusion, of groping in the dark once again, of experiencing many aspects of life and freedom for the first time. Perhaps this observation is not all that incorrect.

If we take a close look at the Church today, we find a Church facing both serious problems and unprecedented opportunities. A product of its own history and the world in which it finds itself, the Church of today faces the crisis to change. Too long has it stood as a bulwark against change—so much so, that this age of change has caused it great pain and stress. When we never exercise certain parts of the body for a long time, it takes a greater effort to revive them.

We can list some of the problems this has caused as a tremendous loss of vocations, a credibility gap in authority, spiritual and moral decay, and the result in financial troubles. Laity and religious alike have departed membership in the Church. Converts are at a minimum. Divisions exist between conservative and liberal factions. The age-old truths are being questioned. Canon law is being dispensed with. The faithful who remain are confused. The answers of centuries are no longer accepted. The Church is experiencing internal and external friction and still there are some who are willing to cover it all up by insisting on a return to those things that (undoubtedly) caused this crisis in the first place. Returning to old, entrenched ideas and philosophies will not solve the future. It will simply perpetuate the past (and there has been too much of that)!

At the same time that all this is happening, there appear on the horizon many opportunities for a fruitful future. No one can disclaim the great work of Biblical scholarship in this age. No age has had a greater relationship between Christians and non-Christians as well. Today's Church is experiencing a revitalized prayer life in countless small communities. New forms of vocations are on the rise. The laity are more involved in the ministry of the Church that is rightly theirs. Diversity is at last being reckoned with. Pluralism is possible. Not since the Middle Ages has there been such a wealth of theological insight and productivity as there has been in this present age of ours.

The things I have mentioned are certainly not all that could be said to describe our Church today, but they depict the turmoil and confusion with which we are faced. However, I think the problems are not insurmountable and the opportunities are possible. One thing is sure—this age of turmoil has forced everyone in the Church (especially the theologians) to re-examine who they are, what the Church is, and who Jesus is.

Given the difficulties of our age and the mistakes of the past, we still pray and hope for a future. Like all living beings, the Church moves toward fulfillment, completion, and perfection—toward a vision of the future—a vision of all people and God, a vision when all people will come to full humanity—a vision of a community for all people despite differences and diversity—a vision of people and God united in the body of Christ.

Ultimately to answer the question, "Who is the Church?" we must say with Scripture that it is all humankind and God together. It seems this is still a vision and not a reality. But the vision is not all that impossible, for it has already begun. We have already experienced God in our existence. God has lived and walked among us in Jesus of Nazareth. We have only to accept or reject him. If we reject him, we shall be no different than the traders and merchants in the temple of fancy, pursuing our own selfish interests. If we accept him then there is a chance for a new world, a new earth, a new heaven, a new Israel and even a new Church! But remember—to accept Jesus includes doing what he did, living as he lived, preaching what he preached, loving as he loved. And whoever does this is "Ecclesia"—the Church of Jesus Christ!

WHAT IS THIS PLACE?

What is this place where we are meeting?
Only a house, the earth its floor,
walls and a roof sheltering people,
windows for light, an open door.
Yet is becomes a body that lives
when we are gathered here
and know our God is near.

Words from afar, stars that are falling,
sparks that are sown in us like seed,
names for our God, dreams signs and wonders
sent from the past are all we need.
We in this place remember and speak
again what we have heard:
God's free redeeming word.

And we accept bread at this table
broken and shared, a living sign.
Here in this world, dying and living,
we are each other's bread and wine.
This is the place where we can receive
what we need to increase
God's justice, love, and peace.

10.
THE IRONY OF CHURCH

Readings: II Chronicles 5:1-14; 6:1-11 Ephesians 2:19-22
Matthew 5:23-24; 7:1-5

You are no longer strangers." "You form a building which rises on the foundation of apostles and prophets." "You are being built into a dwelling-place for God." "You are fellow members of the household of God"—and like most households—you engage in petty battles over rights and privileges; who's right and who's wrong. This is what the author of the Letter to the Ephesians might address to the Church of the third millennium!

St. Paul would come down even stronger on the contemporary Church if he had the chance to send us one of his scathing missives. He would probably say that we are bickering like people who have no faith. He would probably say that the universal Church is being disrupted rather than unified now. Then he would probably continue by reminding us who we are and embarrass the "hell" out of us, showing us how un-Christlike we are and fill us with the awareness of our need to be reconciled with one another!

In the midst of all the politics, power plays, and stone-throwing that is going on today between the Church of Rome and the Church at large, someone has got to call a halt to all of this and return us to the vision! In the wake of silencing theologians, usurping the rights of bishops, and attacking defenseless minorities, Catholics must be getting a rather depressing view of who we are as the Church of Jesus Christ. There is "pro-life" and "pro-choice" who never dialogue. There is a hierarchy who speaks but never listens. There are clergy and laity who build fences between themselves. There are conservative and liberal factions among the clergy and laity who judge rather than ask questions. There are sterile and outdated liturgies, poor homilies, and a legalism that overshadows the mystery of the sacraments. There is a paranoia and a fear of dialogue within that keeps people apart rather than united.

The Scripture leads the way, as always, toward balancing the vision (which I will call *reality*) with the present occurrences in the Church (which I will call *unreality*). The *reality* of who we are as Church is very clear from the Scripture: We are people of the covenant—the mutual response between God and people toward the building of the city of peace (II Chronicles). We are saints and citizens of this city already, the very temple in which God dwells (Ephesians). We are brothers and sisters reconciled to God and therefore to one another in Jesus (Matthew).

The *unreal* condition of the present-day Church is violating this vision, this truth, this reality, this word of God. Once again, a dark cloud has entered the temple. But, perhaps, as in the days of Solomon, God is speaking to us from this dark cloud—a cloud that seems again to be hindering the ministry of the Church as it did in the time of Solomon.

Unlike modern poetry, which posits that behind every dark cloud there is a silver lining, the Hebrew Scripture calls us to find God in the dark cloud and not outside of it. Leave it to the Jews to keep us honest and force us to face the facts rather than run away from them. Some of us want to pray about all this and go to church and plead with God to straighten it all out. In the Gospel, Jesus, another Jew, says no. Jesus says, go and reconcile yourself first, then come and bring your gift to the altar. Then we will begin to see that the greatest gift we can give to one another in our Church today is the gift of forgiveness, of reconciliation, of solving the conflicts that have arisen.

But reconciliation takes a lot of work and energy, and time—most of us have little or none left in this world of ours. Still, we must! It's the only way to return to the vision. Reconciliation means dialogue. Has there been any?

No—mostly one-way communication from Rome to us. We must speak too. We have a responsibility to speak out, to stand up and be counted. And we must do this with the greatest amount of understanding and grace that befits citizens of the Church. Reconciliation means taking a risk. Have you risked anything? Are you willing to be mis-understood or mis-interpreted for the sake of the vision? Just because you reach out doesn't mean you will be received—just because you speak up doesn't mean you'll be listened to—just because you care doesn't mean you'll be accepted. Reconciliation will mean for you what it meant for him whose name you bear—the cross! And the cross is the central image of our vision of Church.

Baptism mounts us on the road to the cross, because the cross is where the Christian meets God—where strangers become brothers and sisters—where the covenant is ratified—where unreality becomes reality—where fact becomes faith—where aliens become Church—where crucifixion becomes exaltation—where dark clouds become a vision—where hate is turned into love—where captivity is liberated—where the dead rise to new life—where the vision becomes a fact!

The time has come for every member of the Church to bear the cross, the cross of conflict—two beams of the same reality going in two different directions and yet forming the image that best describes this reality. For Jesus, the cross was the place where fact and vision intersected. It wasn't until he faced the cross with his total being and gave himself without limit that the vision became clear. Once he faced the cross, he emerged victorious and the vision became a fact. We call that fact the Church, the body of Christ, resurrected and living on in this world, in us, in you and me and the pope and the bishops and the theologians and the pastors and all who have been baptized into Christ Jesus, our Lord and Savior.

So, WHO we are as Church is clear. WHAT we do and HOW we do it will now become proof of WHO WE really are at this moment in history!

Therefore, in the face of the present crisis, the present cross in our Church, I am forced to ask you and myself some very pertinent questions:

1. Are we concerned about all this at all?
2. Have we become informed of the issues at stake?
3. Are we capable of responding to the present conflicts?
4. Have we responded?
5. How?
6. What are we doing to help us return to who we are as Church?
7. How is what we are doing returning us to the vision of Church?

You see, folks—this is your Church, our Church—the Church is you, us!

If **you** don't—if **we** don't—make the vision of Church a fact in our world, who will?

WE HAVE NO GLORY

We have no glory,
we have no name
but the name of Jesus,
the Lord.
We have no glory
but his cross.

Great is the mystery of faith;
he was made public in the flesh
and justified in the spirit
and he appeared to the angels.
He was proclaimed to the people
and found faith here in this world
and he was taken up in glory (I Timothy 3).

If we have died with him,
with him we shall also live.
If we hold firm we shall reign with him,
with him we shall live and reign.
If we deny him, he will deny us.
We may be faithless, he is faithful,
for he cannot deny himself (II Timothy 2).

11.
DIALOGUE—ERROR—EXPERIMENTATION

Readings: Ephesians 4:1-7, 11-16 Luke 21:7-19

Remember the days when priests and religious had to keep silence in their rectories and convents! Remember the days when nuns dressed outrageously differently from the rest of the world! Remember the days when it was a sin to talk in church! Remember incense, novenas, processions, bells, and young girls dressed like little brides, and young boys dressed like little priests! Remember Latin, rosaries, missals, mumbling, and silence! Remember being told not to go into a Protestant church and not even to play with Protestant children! Remember the Syllabus or the Index or the movies and books we were not to partake of! Remember the "good ole days!" Remember your Church—our Church—us—the Church!

If we can remember all these things, then we can remember a world within the world. Then we have lived in the Church of the past few centuries whose pastoral approach had been to create another world within this world, fashioning her own institutions and laws that have isolated the Christian from the rest of humanity. Remember when your non-Catholic friends invited you over to dinner on Friday and fed you meat! Remember on Saturday evenings after a movie or show, you had to starve and watch your friends eat hamburgers, because you had to fast from midnight if you wanted to go to communion on Sunday!

These are all little and unimportant examples I am using, but they point to a very important problem. The problem was and still is the attitude of the Church toward the rest of the world. The attitude of the past few centuries has hindered Church/world dialogue and divorced religion from everyday life in the consciousness of Christians. For a long time theology showed little interest in the development of humanity. It took little account of the new concepts of the universe that were being formulated by other believers and nonbelievers alike. There was a static, if not stagnant, view of God and people. Each element of existence had its place and was properly arranged to lead people to God. Never had such a harmony existed between heaven and earth, time and eternity, the individual and society, state and Church, reason and faith. That world was at the mercy of theologians, and cardinals and bishops manipulated God.

As all this took place, the Church seemed to grow more and more distrustful of the sense and thrust of history. For she conceived as "suspicious" anything and anyone that disrupted her static image of the world. This mistrust prevented the Church from seeing that *changeability* is a permanent category of salvation history. It also prevented her from dialoguing with the world, whose thought became more and more bound up with the process of historical becoming.

This was and is a calamity for the Church, because the Church defines herself as giving service to and dialoguing with the world. The world sets the agenda for the Church and not the other way around. The Church should serve the world and not the other way around.

There has been a long gap in Church/world dialogue. Vatican II ended that gap "in principle." It is now up to us to end it "in deed." Because of our past, we are still shaky about dialoguing with nonbelievers. We are just as shaky while dialoguing with those of our own faith, especially when we think they will disagree with what we believe. May I offer a possible pattern for our behavior in this regard? In Ephesians, we heard that there is one Spirit, but many spiritualities—many ways of living the Christian life. This idea of spirituality is intimately linked with faith and dialogue. For there is one faith, but it is lived in many different ways. And that faith cannot be defined once and for all by any one person, any one pope, or any one church in a given age. It is a lifetime process for every human being and a lifetime process for every church in every age. Even more so, it is an eternal process for all humanity and the body of Christ. What I am saying is this: It is the spirituality of some to keep silence. It is the spirituality of others to dialogue. Both are prayer!

Both are expressions of the same faith! Both are inspired by the same Spirit! We have come of age. There is a new asceticism in the Church. Even those who live a life of community prayer and silence find place for dialogue. And those who have been active and dialoguing in the Church are maturing and growing more in this spirituality!

What exactly does it mean to dialogue? What does one do when one dialogues? Dialogue is communicating between two or more persons. The purpose of this communication is mutual. The outcome of this communication is growth and the furtherance of the truth. Dialoguing is testing our truth. It is not where one person has something to give another—it is not just dispensing our ideas on another. The purpose of dialogue is to raise the question for yourself and the other. It is in raising the question that you both begin to possess the truth. There is a difference in knowing the truth and dialoguing to find out that something is true. For to formulate a truth in words and to really possess it are two distinct things. For example, we read from the Scripture and believe with all our hearts that "God is love." Now, this is an undeniable truth. But is the truth really possessed by a Christian who is prejudiced against Negroes or whites or Jews or women? Dialogue becomes, then, a means for seeking the truth. Possessing the truth and seeking the truth are not opposed courses. They are essentially related. The truth we possess is constantly in danger of becoming mere words if we do not flesh it out in dialogue. And dialogue is a way of seeking the truth.

Dialogue is education, although it is not a lecture or a sermon. Dialogue is seeking to build community and not "chit-chat" or conversation between community dwellers. Dialogue is a wedge where something new grows out of the old. Dialogue is not giving answers or being unloving and unrelenting, with the attitude "you have your opinion, I have mine." Dialogue is in essence openness, reaching out, sharing, giving and taking, learning, loving, losing oneself in the other. Dialogue is looking at oneself in the light of the questions raised, remembering that it is never we who raise the questions, but life that raises the questions.

Dialogue is also a risk—many times it is problematic. Dialogue makes us vulnerable and can cause division—"you will be arrested and persecuted; you will be handed over to trial...you will be handed over by your parents, your brothers, your relatives, and your friends." Even though we realize this possibility, we still cringe from being the cause of conflict. Perhaps this is why so many people remain apathetic and complacent. It's easier to be silent than to get involved and dialogue. Yet for those who do get involved, who do experience rejection and persecution, who are involved in meaningful confrontations, the words of Jesus ring true: "Don't be afraid when you hear of wars and revolutions; such things must happen first, but they do not mean that the end is near." He who walked this way first and calls us in his footsteps has said, "Everyone will hate you because of me."

No one claims that dialogue is an easy way out, just as no one claims the Christian life is easy. However, it is like a glimpse of the sun, a green twig in winter. It is our only hope! Dialogue is the light that leads the world away from the silence of death. And as long as human words are spoken, as long as we are willing to listen to each other and understand, then there will be a Church—a Church who serves this world—and together with this world will become the truth!

AS LONG AS THERE ARE MEN AND WOMEN

As long as there are men and women,
as long as earth has fruit to give,
so long are you our loving God that
we thank you for all things that live.

As long as human words are spoken,
as long as people understand,
so long will you be here among us
we give you thanks in Jesus' name.

You feed the birds, you clothe the flowers,
you know your creatures and their ways.
O God, you are my home, my refuge,
and in your hands are all my days.

You are our light, we go on living,

you lead the world away from death.
You sent your only son to save us—
   his body is our living bread.

So everything your love has granted
must worship you while life endures.
You came to live your life among us,
O God, we know that we are yours.

12.
THE GREETING OF PEACE

The gesture of the greeting of peace is as old as the Eucharist itself! But even as the Eucharist has its origin in a more ancient custom (that of breaking bread) so too the greeting of peace has a more ancient origin in the spontaneous gesture of people greeting each other in ancient cultures, even in public.

In Christian usage, the greeting of peace finds its origin in the Scripture itself. John's Gospel echoes this gesture as Jesus promises his disciples, "Peace is my farewell to you, my peace is my gift to you" (John 14:27). The city of Jerusalem is traditionally called the "city of peace." (This city witnessed the peace and reconciliation between the Jewish and Gentile Christians in the early Church.) "Shalom" is the central Easter gift of Jesus to the Church. "Shalom" is the spirit of the Christ. "Shalom" is the cornerstone of the Church.

As early as the letters of St. Paul, the greeting or kiss of peace is a common gesture practiced within the Christian community. Paul himself uses the greeting thirty times in his letters, Luke uses it seventeen times, and we find it described in twenty-seven other locations in the letters of the Christian Testament (e.g., I Peter 5:14). How was it described? In the earliest writing of the Christian Testament, Paul urges the Christians at Thessalonica, "Greet all the brothers and sisters with a holy kiss" (I Thess.5:26). He repeats this exhortation in almost every letter he writes (Romans 16:16, I Corinthians 16:20, II Corinthians 13:12, etc.).

The four Gospels, on numerous occasions, refer to the "kiss" of peace. Two striking occasions are when Jesus reprimands Simon the Pharisee, by saying, "You did not give me a kiss, but this woman has not ceased kissing my feet since the time I entered" (Luke 7:45). And in the garden of Gethsemane, Jesus says to Judas, one of his apostles, "Judas, are you betraying the Son of People with a kiss" (Luke 22:48)?

From the Scripture alone, we are taught the sacredness of this gesture. This gesture unites us, it does not divide us!

Throughout the centuries, the Church retained the kiss of peace in one form or another as part of its liturgy. In the Mass at the time of Justin Martyr, approximately 150 CE, we find this written following the Liturgy of the Word, "When the prayers are finished, we give each other a kiss." Tertullian, in one of his writings, notes that in ancient Christian practice, the kiss of peace was looked upon as the "seal" put on prayer. In approximately 380 CE, in the Apostolic Constitution, the greeting was moved from being the conclusion to the Liturgy of the Word to introducing the Eucharistic Prayer. Here is its description:
- Next the deacon says: Let us all attend.
- The bishop then greets the assembly saying: The peace of God be with you all.
- The people reply: And with thy spirit.
- The deacon says to all: Greet one another with a holy kiss.
- The clergy then give the kiss (of peace) to the bishop, laymen give it to laymen, and women to women.

In the year 416 CE, Pope Innocent I, in his letter to the bishop of Gubbio, advocates putting the kiss of peace before communion, where it is located in the present Roman Rite. There was a gradual change in this gesture over the years from a free exchange by all to a regimented order of who can kiss whom by the tenth century, and even to a thing called the "osculatorium" or "kissing board" or "pax board" in the thirteenth century—each person received the board in turn, kissed it, and passed it on.

And so, over the centuries, this gesture has undergone many alterations, yet it never ceased to be a vital and central gesture of the Christian liturgy. Even before Vatican II, even though the faithful never engaged in the gesture, it remained a clerical gesture in pontifical and solemn high Masses when more than one cleric was present.

Since its restoration by Vatican II to its original free exchange by all the baptized, the American culture has welcomed this gesture with much openness and diversity. Every Catholic congregation (and some Protestant ones also) has its own style. My intention is not to comment on any particular style, nor to critique anyone's views of this gesture, but to present an objective analysis of this gesture gleaned from Scripture, history, and theology.

Having done the first two (Scripture and history), let me conclude with the third—theology. The best way of doing this is by telling you what theology says the greeting of peace is NOT and then what our theology says it IS.

First, what it is NOT:

The greeting of peace is not a time for conversation or gossip or settling some business with someone. It is not a time for pastoral care or an extension of the homily or Liturgy of the Word. The greeting of peace should not be the time when we criticize someone—their ideas or their dress. It is not a time for questions and answers, talking about "things," nor is it a time for a lot of words. The greeting of peace is not a time to be greeted, nor a time for standing still or with a closed posture. It is not necessarily a time to reach everyone, or a time to avoid people. It is not a ritual. It is not an intermission.

And now, what it IS:

The greeting of peace is tradition, remembrance, gesture, prayer, and liturgy. It is the experience of a dream, a wish, a hope, a desire, a vision, and a promise. It is outreach and encounter. It is a time to greet. It is the fullest expression of presence, healing, touch, and grace. The greeting of peace is a time for sincerity, being genuine, saying hello and good-bye. It is a moment of respect, a moment when your arms are open, when you move and visit. It is an exercise of sexuality, a handshake, a kiss, an embrace, liturgical dance. The greeting of peace is a moment of relief, a time for relaxation and refreshment, a time for tears and laughter, a time for intermingling, contacting and engaging people, a real intermezzo.

Lastly, this greeting or kiss is a gift—it is God's gift to Jesus, it is

Jesus' gift to the Church, it is the Church's gift to the world, it is the gift the world cannot give to itself. Then let **us** bring that gift to the world, but first, let us bring that gift to one another inside the church: Peace—Shalom—May the peace of the risen Christ be with you now and forever. Amen!

(With acknowledgment to Josef Jungmann, SJ, and his book, *The Mass*; and *Early Sources of the Liturgy* by Lucien Deiss, CSSp.)

FOR PEACE

Far too late have I begun to love you;
beauty, you are so old and yet so new.

Far too late have I begun to love you;
you were there within me, I was outside,
and I sought you, seeing blindly just beyond myself;
and poured away like water,
I took flight from you and I was lost,
surrounded by such beauty which is not you.

Then you called and cried aloud to me,
breaking through the silence of my deafness.
Dazzling brightness, you appeared to me,
and at once you put to flight my blindness.
Drawing deep, I smell your fragrant presence;
still I gasp for breath and long for you.
Since I tasted you, I only thirst and hunger after you.
How, with a simple touch, your fire consumes me.
Now my heart, aflame and blazing, leaps to you for peace.

13.
HALLOWEEN—ALL SAINTS—ALL SOULS

Readings: Revelation 7:2-4, 9-14 I John 3:1-3 Matthew 5:1-12

The feast of All Saints stands in the middle of two other celebrations in our Church—Halloween or All Hallows Eve which is celebrated the night before and All Souls' Day which is celebrated on the day after. I am putting all three of these holydays in this one sermon to show you how related they really are and why this is all one festival in three parts!

Vesting or costuming in strange garments from those you normally wear has always been seen as a gesture of taking on a new identity. Sometimes that identity is funny or serious or scary or silly or meaningful or mysterious. But it is always a new identity from the one we normally have. We often complete that new identity by changing our voice or wearing a mask to depict that new identity in its entirety. Where this idea or custom comes from and why it is still done will become more or less clear as I go on with this sermon.

What we are doing these three days is older than Christianity itself. It is the recognition of some basic human facts that go back to the beginning of time. We recognize that we are not alone—we, the living, are not the beginning of existence—life does not begin with me—existence is older than the present generation of people. What we have today in this world is not only our own doing, but also the work of generations of people who have gone before us. We stand in their shoes! We stand where our ancestors stood! Our ancestors are dead!

The recognition of this fact by our ancestors developed into mask wearing and costuming. At Halloween, we continue that tradition by gesturing the presence of the dead in our midst with masks, costumes, and trinkets.

The history of this custom is vague and varied throughout the ages. Perhaps it all started with the basic need to remember the dead, but in a more dramatic way than just with our memories. Masks were probably the first expression. Costumes came later. And finally even the need for anonymity by voice changing. The oldest form of Halloween we know of is the one where people believed that if they wore a mask depicting someone who was dead—that dead person would be alive and present again in the person wearing the mask. This gesture was also part of the ancient Greek theatre where masks hid the identity of the actor in favor of the character. So, all in all, Halloween (or whatever it was called back then) came first.

When Christianity came along and emerged as a world religion, it made a habit of transforming already existing rituals and celebrations—Christianizing them—reshaping them with Christian theology. Thus emerged the feast of All Saints (a remembrance of the unknown and unnamed and uncanonized saints in heaven) and the feast of All Souls' (a remembrance of all the dead whether they were saints or not). All Saints' was celebrated on November 1 and All Souls' on November 2. We can tell from these dates that the earlier rituals and celebrations were held on or around the same time of the year—the fall—when life ripens and dies! Since the Church was never in the practice of suppressing non-Christian rituals, but rather transforming them, the emergence of Halloween (All Hallows Eve or the eve before All Saints') became inevitable on October 31.

Therefore, as you can see, all three celebrations are related: Halloween—All Saints'—All Souls'!

What we Catholics do is not satanic or evil or wrong—as some would have you believe. What we do these three days is *Godlike, holy*, and *just*! *Godlike*—because we believe the dead are with God; concealed in God; God is a mask on the land of the dead; God is the safe place where the dead rest in peace. *Holy*—because death is a part of life; it will come to us as well; when it does, we hope someone will remember us; this is holistic, whole, and holy to see that life and death are two sides of the same mystery—the mystery we celebrate these three days—the mystery of ourselves! *Just*—because remembering is a sacred act, the oldest act on earth; we do justice to all those who have gone before us, to their lives, their work, their meaning, their worth as we call them forth from the dead into our midst.

So—awake you who sleep in death…
Remove your mask, O God…
Be here among us…
Saints, sinners, Christians, and all who have died…
Bring us to life!

AWAKE YOU WHO SLEEP

Awake, you who sleep,
rise up from the dead
and Christ will be your light.

We wait for the light,
but it remains dark,
for the light of the sun,
but we walk in darkness.
Like blind people
we grope along the wall,
uncertain, like people
without eyes.
We stumble in broad daylight,
in the prime of our lives
we are like the dead.

Arise, shine, your light
has come.
For the glory of God
breaks forth over you.
God is a mantle of light
around you.
God will name you:

"No-longer-abandoned."
At night you will no longer
need the moon,
for Yahweh-God will be
your light.

Be here among us,
light in the midst of us.
Come to our rescue
bring us to life.
God in the midst of us,
Jesus Messiah.
Light of the world,
come here among us.
You are the living one,
source of our life.
Come to our rescue,
Son of God.

Awake, you who sleep,
rise up from the dead
and Christ will be your light.

14.
SANCTITY

Readings: Revelation 7:2-4, 9-14 Psalm 24 I John 3:1-3
Matthew 5:1-12

How does the Scripture above define a saint?

"The servants of our God…a huge crowd that no one could count from every race, people, and tongue…dressed in long white robes and holding palm branches…ones who have survived the great period of trial…they who have washed their robes and made them white in the blood of the lamb" (Revelation).

"Those whose hands are sinless and whose heart is clean, who desire not what is vain" (Psalm 24).

"Children of God…pure" (I John).

"Poor in spirit…sorrowing…lowly…those who hunger and thirst for holiness…they who show mercy…the singled hearted…peacemakers… those persecuted for holiness' sake…those who are insulted, persecuted, and slandered because of their faith" (Matthew).

Quite a mouthful! If this is the definition of a saint, I don't think any of us will make it!

Yet, if I look at that definition again—I believe I know many saints. For a saint is not someone who is all those things, but someone who is just one of those things, lived to perfection.

And what exactly is perfection? Perfection is being complete—whole (holy)! And being complete is being who I am with all my imperfections.

It is the saying of holy people (of saints) that, if we wish to be perfect, we have nothing more to do than to perform well the ordinary duties of life.

Living life to the full is the road to sanctity. Going through the process of life is the surest road to perfection. It is not the easiest, but it is the surest. It is a process of birth, death, rebirth, seven times and seven times over—of allowing ourselves to be thrown in the fiery furnace, to be unmasked, to be squeezed so small, to sell everything we have, become naked, a child, a seed in the ground.

This is the process of all life, not just human life. This is the process that everyone we call a saint has gone through. If we wish to become a saint (and who doesn't!) we must be willing to live life this way. This is the way of the Gospel—the way of Jesus, who asks us to take up our cross daily—not his cross—but **our** cross—whatever, wherever, and whenever that may be.

If we are willing to do this, then for us, like every saint before us: "Seventy times seven trees will blossom where our home is standing. Light will stream upon the waters!"

SEVEN TIMES

Seven times, seven times
born anew as a little child
squeezed so small, driven out
into life to be a human.

Seventy times
seven trees
will blossom
where our home
is standing.
Light will stream
upon the waters…

Seven times, seven times
born anew as a little child
squeezed so small, driven out
into life to be a human.

15.
MARY OF NAZARETH

Readings: Revelation 11:19a; 12:1-6a, 10 Psalm 45:10-12, 16 I Corinthians 15:20-27 Luke 1:39-56

On November 1, 1950 (the feast of All Saints), in the square of Vatican City, Pope Pius XII declared the Assumption of Mary into heaven, calling her "The Queen of Heaven and Earth." In the Litany of Loretto we hear the sonorous and beautiful titles given Mary, such as "Mother of Good Counsel," "Morning Star," "Seat of Wisdom." Over the centuries, there have been innumerable portraits and representations of Mary in art, from Botticelli to Raphael. We have experienced the efforts of preachers and writers who feel that ordinary language is inadequate to describe this heavenly woman. From the Bible she is given such titles as "Lily of Israel," "Daughter of the Princes of Judah," "Mother of All the Living."

All of this seems to place the person of Mary of Nazareth so much above us and so far beyond our reach. But she was also a peasant woman, a Jewish peasant woman, the wife of a working man. Like every woman in the tiny village of first-century Nazareth, her hands were scored with labor; her feet dusty with the hard stinging grit from tracks that led to the well…to the olive gardens…to the synagogue. Mary lived the routine and daily life of any other Jewish woman of the common people.

It is so easy for us to praise the "Mother of God"—to ask her to pray for us—to raise her to great dignity—and just as easy to lose sight of the reasons we would do such things.

That she should be the mother of her creator is certainly a high dignity, yet this is not why the Church pays her such homage. It is her virtue that we consider—her love and endurance—her humility and purity—her patience and meekness—her ability to suffer in silence—her openness to the mystery of life—her humanness. She imitated her son, Jesus, so closely in life that the Church believes with all its might that she has been rewarded in the same manner as her son. Jesus rose from the dead to show us our destiny. Mary shares in this resurrection because she lived her life according to God's Word. Mary is the sign to us that all will be raised to life in Christ.

Her message to us is a simple one: Become human! That is what we have been called to do. Just live life as you find it, where you find it. Become a mirror of justice; a cause for someone's joy; health for the sick; comforter of the afflicted—and know that this is what it means to be human!

16.
IMMACULATE CONCEPTION

Readings: Genesis 3:9-15, 20 Ephesians 1:3-6, 11-12 Luke 1:26-38

The Immaculate Conception—Mary conceived without sin! Is that possible? Is it possible to escape the original sin of Adam and Eve? Isn't sin part of the human condition? Is it possible to be born without sin and still be human?

These questions haunt us who believe in the Immaculate Conception. These questions bug us because they are about sin. This dogma makes us squirm when we realize that the world is racked with sin all around us (both individual and communal sin) and that there are very few virgins left in our society.

Then, let us briefly reflect on these questions.

Is it possible to be born without sin and still be human? You hear many people say they are sinners because they are human. We are used to equating those words with one another—sin and human. But this dogma says otherwise—it says you are not human when you sin, you are inhuman! Being human includes the possibility of sin, but sinning is not the essence of what it means to be human. Therefore, it is possible to be born without sin and still be human. For to be human is not to sin, not to live for yourself; not to be prejudiced, apathetic, envious, greedy, unjust, unloving, unwilling, close-minded, and captive. But being human is to be open, a servant, living for others, free, giving of yourself totally; filled with hope, faith, and love; aware of the diversity in others and loving them the way they are.

The second question asks, isn't sin part of the human condition?

Of course! Who would deny that! But, as I mentioned above, it is not essential to the human condition. Are not faith, hope, love, courage, strength, beauty, and goodness also part of the human condition? Which is more essential to being human, good or evil? Which one in the end will overcome? The answers to these questions are ours to give!

The third and last question asks, is it possible to escape the original sin of Adam and Eve? In every one of us there is the potential of good and evil. In the Bible this fact is portrayed in many stories. However, the story that best portrays the evil side of the human condition is the story of Adam and Eve. The stories that best portray the good side of the human condition are the Gospels. In the Gospels we find two characters who not only balance out the human condition, but who, in their very lives, become the fulfillment of what it means to be human—Jesus and Mary! Of them, it is said: They were without sin! Of them, it is said: They were completely human! We call Jesus, the new Adam, and Mary, the new Eve. Adam and Eve stand as symbols of the old creation—that part of us that is sinful and inhuman. Jesus and Mary stand as symbols of the new creation—that part of us that is human, redeemed, and free.

In every one of us, there is a little bit of Adam and Eve and a little bit of Jesus and Mary—a little bit of evil and a little bit of good.

Which is the real me?

Which is the real you?

Which does it take to become human?!

17.
JOSEPH OF NAZARETH

Now the birth of Jesus the Messiah took place in this way. When his mother Mary had been engaged to Joseph, but before they lived together, she was found to be with child…
(Matthew 1:18).

DENIAL—ISOLATION—NUMBING—SHOCK
(Calmly)

This isn't really happening! I can't believe Miriam would do such a thing!

(Pause/stare)

There must be some logical explanation—Miriam's logic, however, is no logic at all. I ask her whose child it is—she says she doesn't know. I ask her was she raped—she says "no." I ask her if she consented to this adultery—she says it wasn't adultery. I ask her how it happened—she says again she doesn't know.

(Pause)

What are people going to say about this? I'll never be able to face the village again!

(Pause)

Maybe we're not even betrothed legally—that would solve it!—I'll check with the elders in the morning. Maybe there's a hitch and I can get out of this betrothal.

ANGER—YEARNING AND SEARCHING FOR THE LOST—DEFENSIVE RETREAT

(Slowly getting angry)

I wonder if she loves the person who got her pregnant and is trying to protect him! What about me! What about protecting me! Does this mean she doesn't even love me? We've been promised to each other for years. She's my property—I paid for her—I expected a virgin.

My honor is at stake! My posterity is at stake! My opportunity to observe the Law and become a father are shattered! She's carrying someone else's child! This child will not perpetuate my life on earth. For me, there will be no eternal life in this pregnancy. My hopes and visions have all come to a "dead end."

What good is there in being an observant Jew anyway? Apparently, even God betrays his own! Not even the upright can make any claims on the God of the covenant. What is the covenant anyway if God does not play his part?

BARGAINING
(Long pause)

Perhaps, I'm not as upright and observant as I think? Maybe I've done something wrong and this is God's punishment on me?

(Praying)

My spirit is broken, O God, my days are extinct.

Surely there are mockers around me, and my eye dwells on their provocation.

My eye has grown dim from grief, and all my members are like a shadow.

The upright are appalled at this, and the innocent stir themselves up against the godless.

Yet the righteous hold to their way, and they that have clean hands grow stronger and stronger.

My days are past, my plans are broken off, the desires of my heart.

Have pity on me, O God, and make known to me my transgression so that I may repent and be restored to honor in your sight and the sight of all the people (Job 17).

DEPRESSION—DISORIENTATION/DESPAIR—
ACKNOWLEDGMENT
(Subdued)

This is too much to bear!

I thought I knew Miriam. She's the daughter of my father's cousin. We grew up together. I never thought she could do such a thing!

My trust in her is gone. My trust in God is gone. Who can I trust? Who can I turn to?

It's a problem I have no solution for—yet it is I who must solve it!

I don't really know what to do next!

ACCEPTANCE—REORIENTATION—ADAPTATION
(Resigned)

Apparently: I need to "let go" of my pride—it happened—it's over. I need to "let go" of my heritage—it's not my child. I need to "let go" of my expectations—she won't be my wife. I need to "let go" of my feelings! What about Miriam?—her pride, her heritage, her feelings, her dilemma?

I must do what is best for both of us. I must also "let go" of my love for her. The Law will carry me through. The righteous act is what will save us.

In my heart, I can find no way to solve this—my affections and emotions don't help—they are not as solid as the Law. I will do what the Law permits, because it is who I am and what will be best for both of us!

Therefore, in the morning, I will seek out the elders and quietly divorce her without exposing her to the Law. Yes, that's what will be best. For if I expose Miriam, I expose myself as well.

This is the only way I can deal with all this!

But just when he had resolved to do this, an angel of the Lord appeared to him in a dream and said, "Joseph, son of David, do not be afraid to take Mary as your wife, for the Child conceived in her is from the Holy Spirit. She will bear a son, and you are to name him, Jesus, for he will save his people from their sins." All this took place to fulfill what has been spoken by the Lord through the prophet: "Look, the virgin shall conceive and bear a son, and they shall name him Emmanuel," which means, "God is with us." When Joseph awoke from sleep... (Matthew 1:20-24)

POST DREAM
(Awaking)

What was that all about?!

Whoa!

I thought sleep might help—but it's only added this dream to further confuse the issue.

What was that dream anyway? Let me sort it out…I can't seem to remember it exactly…It's very vague and unclear…Somehow I remember that it had something to do with my dilemma…yet blurred and elusive…

(Confused—searching)

The dream somehow suggested another direction than the one I decided on before I went to sleep. The dream offered another possibility. The dream—even though it's not clear—seems to be pointing to some other solution. I want out and the dream urges me to play a part in this. The dream is seductive. It could be an illusion, a result of my stress. What exactly does the dream want me to do?

(Pause—and then quickly)

Interpreting a dream can be dangerous or fruitful. My great ancestor and namesake, Yosef, is a perfect example. Once, his interpretation got him into trouble. Another time his interpretation brought him fame. What will it be for me? Do I dare pursue this dream—or is the dream pursuing me? Am I so arrogant as to think I can interpret as well as my ancestor? Is the dream real? Will following it make me look more foolish than I look already? Is this dream a trick? Do I dare follow it?

(Pursuing)

Let me see—let me remember what I think it was saying: Miriam's pregnancy could be something other than what it appears to be on the surface. There's more to this than meets the eye! My arrogance could be in the way of seeing more to it. OK—what more is there to see?

(More insight)

The dream suggested the work of God in our history—that God works and moves where and how one least expects.

(Getting sensible)

The dream is forcing me to see the hand of God in Miriam's pregnancy—especially since she finds it hard to explain herself. Well, look at our history—look at the Torah—look at Tamar and Ruth and Rahab and the wife of Uriah. Every one of those situations was also scandalous, yet God used them to further his plan for the perpetuating of Israel.

(Skepticism)

Is that what this dream is suggesting? That this pregnancy could be the work of God? That somehow, I would be refusing to participate in God's work in history? The dream suggests that this too is a moment of grace and I must choose wisely.

(Pause)

Do I follow my gut feeling from last evening? Or do I follow the dream I had this morning?

(Long pause)

The Bible says: (Joseph) did as the angel of the Lord commanded him; he took (Miriam) as his wife, but had no marital relations with her until she had borne a son, whom he named Jesus *(Matthew 1:25).*

18.
CHRISTIANITY

Readings: Numbers 21:4-9 Psalm 118 Philippians 2:6-11 John 3:13-17

In the Book of Numbers, in the desert, we find an impatient, wandering, disgusted tribe of Israelites. We find a people searching, fantasizing, not facing up to what life has brought them (hunger, weariness, thirst, frustration, loneliness). In punishment for their complaining, Yahweh sent death, but at the same time relented through Moses by giving him the power to save those who wished to believe.

Since that time, Israel has become an adult person, putting aside its childish fantasies. Its adult testimony is to a God who thinks thoughts of peace, not of destruction, just as a grown person who learns from the experiences of life, and no longer believes in violence, in fighting and winning, in striking and punishing, but in patience and forgiveness. This mature testimony is to a God who no longer forces, who is more and more modest and powerless. This God accompanies people into exile—God's people—God's sons and daughters—and yet they are banished, belittled, and destroyed. There is no more temple and no more prophets like Moses, and God is silent. Only a wretched little group, a remnant in Israel, still recognizes this God. Among them, the expectation is born that this God will ultimately be made known and speak in the form of a servant—someone who does not demand anything from you, who bears and suffers.

That God (says Paul in the Letter to the Philippians) who humiliates and empties himself to give freedom to people—who does not want to fight people, but serve them—that God appeared and spoke in Jesus of Nazareth—Jesus, a Jew, a son of people, one of many people, without form or splendor. He lives and fails, falling into the hands of people. He dies—on a cross—because of a foolish misunderstanding.

Now, if the God of Israel has spoken "forever" in Jesus, and he is called God's Word to this world, then, what is that God making known to us? That God does not demand anything from us. That God wants to liberate and serve us, make no more demands, does not want any sacrifices, does not want to see any blood. That God prefers people to lose God and forget God rather than be bowed down before. That God wants to disappear and be dead, so that we may live!

And it is precisely because of this that we cannot forget God, but will always remember God in our memory of Jesus of Nazareth, God's Son.

It is not just with our memories that we remember Jesus, but also by the way we live—we call it: Christianity—named after his way of life, the way, the truth, and the life. Being a Christian means being called to imitate Jesus' fidelity to the human condition. Being Christian means to challenge death wherever it presents itself, above all when it is the result of inability or refusal to love. Loving with the love of Jesus means loving another in full recognition of his or her otherness—even across all the barriers that people never cease to build between themselves. It means loving down to the very roots of hostility and sin that make an enemy of the other—creating unity at the precise point of alienation. It means embracing the suffering that rejection by the other will bring—the sentence to death for having loved—the actual dying.

The ultimate way of living out this thing called "Christianity" is by giving service in some form of ministry. Ministry is the emptying of oneself to make room for others. Ministry is being open to the service of one's fellow human beings. Ministry is exercising one's commitment as a baptized Christian. Ministry is an opportunity to experience Christianity at its deepest level. Ministry is an imitation of the life of Jesus, making that life and grace present in the world of today.

At one point in his life, Scripture tells us that Jesus said, "The Son of People has not come to be served, but to serve,"—that is, to the point of laying down his life. And when we live this way, when we give witness to his memory, we experience what it means to live, to be human. It is not some religious act that makes a Christian what he or she is, but rather participation in the sufferings of God in the life of the world. This kind of living gives hope—this kind of love is victorious—for this kind of suffering and death is productive of life—for Jesus also said "Whoever wishes to save one's life must lose it"—to die is to live—the paradox of life that we Christians not only believe in, but must live out.

In the story of Jesus from the Bible, all of this is called: the cross! The cross + the place where God and people meet! The cross + the place where I know who I am and what it means to be human! The cross + the place where a person becomes God! The cross + the place where God becomes human! The cross + the sign of a Christian.

ONE WHO GIVES

One who will not
give his life,
one who will not share it
with a multitude
or with even one,
forlorn shall he be.
One who gives
what she has,
she shall live,
eaten up,
and she shall know
at last she's born.

19.
THE MYSTERY OF FAITH

Readings: Habakkuk 1:2-3; 2:2-4 Psalm 25 II Timothy 1:6-8,
13-14 Luke 17:5-10

What do you believe in? Do you believe in a better world? Do you believe in people? Do you believe in God? Do you believe in everything the Church teaches? Do you believe the pope is infallible? Do you believe that Jesus rose from the dead? Do you believe in Heaven? Hell? Purgatory? Limbo? What do you believe in? My guess is that each and every one of us believes something different about each question I just asked! My guess is that we are no different than the apostles in the Gospel: mixed up—uncertain—too certain—confused—absolutely sure of ourselves—having no answer—having all the answers—not really caring—going around with our eyes and ears closed and our mouths open. Are we like the apostles in the Gospel? Do we hinder faith rather than support it? Do we keep people from faith because we'll believe in anything?

Faith is believing. Faith is a way of living. Faith is a direction in life with commitment. If we really believe, then we can never be mixed up. If we really believe, then we must expect to doubt. If we really believe then we do not know. This is the challenge Jesus puts to the apostles when he quips, "If you had faith even the size of a tiny almost invisible mustard seed." Occasionally someone will ask me, "Father, is there a God?" and my answer usually surprises them because I always say, "I don't know." Then they will usually ask me, "Then why are you a priest? And why is there a Church?" And my answer is, "Because I **believe,** and those who also **believe** (as I do) form a community of faith which is the Church."

We who believe are called "the Church"—the Church—you and me—believers. The believer is a person who can stand up and with open eyes entrust oneself to another or many others. Taking others on trust, letting yourself be touched and called, appealed to by others, allowing yourself to be taught by and being amenable to what comes to you, having the courage to expect something from another person, this is faith! Believing is taking a risk and only experience will prove whether it is human and humane. You have to try it out and live it. Believing is intimately related to growing and maturity. Believing is not saying yes with your head lowered and your eyes shut. Believing is making do with what there is, taking the facts seriously, believing your eyes. But it is also being rebellious, "disbelieving," and not putting up with the situation as you find it. Such was the faith of the Prophet Habakkuk who cried out to God against violence and misery, destruction and strife.

What being a believer is and how it works becomes clear in the way people call, pray, and live with each other. There are different ways of believing, just as there are very many different generations and types of people. Faith, then, is where one person respects the other person and leaves that person in freedom to follow his or her own way.

Faith is keeping the group together as Timothy was exhorted to do. Faith is learning to live with one's exact opposite, the person who votes against you. Faith is learning that life is more powerful than any doctrine or dogma. Accepting life as we find it and living it to the full, this is faith!

To make this a better life for all takes a deep faith and a strong commitment. For the Christian, it means to leave **all** things and to follow Jesus.

I SHALL BE LIVING

It will be at the breaking dawn, as then.
The stone is rolled away.
I have risen from the earth.
My eyes can endure the daylight.
I walk and do not stumble.
I speak and understand myself.

People are approaching me,
we find that we know each other.

It will be at the breaking dawn, as then.
The morning mist dissolves.
A barren plain I thought I would see.
Full sheaves I see,
tall with sturdy stalk,
rich in golden grain,
trees that border the farm land,
hills that wave to the distant sky,
sweep upwards and soar to the cloud line.

Beyond this,
as crystal dazzling and blinding,
the sea that gave back her dead.

We pass the night in each other's shadow.
We are awakened by the light of dawn.
As if someone has called us
by our true name.

I shall be living!

20.
GOING BEYOND THE FACTS

Readings: Jeremiah 31:7-9 Psalm 126 Hebrews 5:1-6 Mark 10:46-52

I mmediately, he received his sight and started to follow him up the road."

Mark contrasts the blind man with the regular followers of Jesus. Jesus' regular disciples scold the blind man for his faith. The blind man, who is on the fringe of society, is the one with authentic faith in Jesus. The disciples who are with Jesus all the time show a lack of faith. Jesus commends the faith of the blind man. It is of the blind man that the Gospel says, "Immediately, he received his sight and started to follow Jesus."

The contrast is obvious: the blind see—the seeing are blind!

What does the blind man see? And what is it that the seeing cannot see?

Faith is the key to the Gospel message. The ability to believe is the ability to see what physical sight obscures. Too often, what we look for in life is right in front of our eyes—yet we cannot see it. It takes a new set of eyes to see what the blind man saw, because he had no physical sight. Yet he saw what the disciples still did not see.

Faith is going **beyond** the facts:
- The **fact** is that the blind cannot see!
- **Faith** says the blind can see!
- The **fact** is the seeing can see!
- **Faith** says the seeing are blind!

In the Old Testament it is modeled this way in the Prophet Jeremiah:

- The **fact** is that Israel was in exile in Babylon!
- **Faith** says they would return to the land of Israel!
- The **fact** is that Israel was held captive!
- **Faith** says that Israel is free!

In the New Testament it is modeled this way in the Letter to the Hebrews:

- The **fact** is that Jesus was human!
- **Faith** says that Jesus is divine!
- The **fact** is that Jesus died on a cross!
- **Faith** says that Jesus is risen from the dead!

Do **you** have enough faith to go **beyond** the facts in your life?

PEOPLE OF GOD

Not like a storm or a flood,
not like a blow to the tree trunk
comes every word of our God,
not like a shot in the heart.

But like a glimpse of the sun
like a green twig in the winter
thirsty and hard is this ground—
such is the kingdom of God.

Word like a slave in our midst
voice that encircles the silence
name with no ring, with no force
stranger without any race.

Those who are hounded by peace
children and those poor in spirit
hear that name sound in their hearts
shoulder the word in their flesh.

Even the blind know this hand
deaf ones and mute understand it
happy the one who believes
happy the tree near the spring.

Not in the tomb of the past
nor in the temple of fancy—
God is right here in our midst
here in the shadow of hope.

God becomes worthy of trust
here in this life that is dying.
We become people of God—
love more than life, more than death.

21.
THREE WORLD RELIGIONS

Readings: Genesis 9:8-15 I Peter 3:18-22 Mark 1:12-15

"See, I am now establishing my covenant with you and your descendents after you."

A covenant is an agreement or a contract that is mutual between two parties. However, a covenant is not something legal, such as signing a check. For when you sign a check, it's done. Nor is it like buying a house—for once the house is yours, the former owner has no more claims to make on it and no more responsibilities toward you. A covenant is not a one-time transaction, but it is a lived experience between two parties. (For example, as two people who get married—to fulfill the covenant of marriage, one must do more than sign a marriage license or promise vows in church. One must live out the covenant day in and day out for better or for worse.)

Certainly, then, we can see how our baptism is a covenant. For it has no meaning just because some priest or deacon poured water over our head, or our parents and godparents signed a certificate stating that they witnessed our baptism. The covenant of baptism gets its meaning, its fulfillment, only from how we live each day according to the promises we made.

All throughout the Old Testament there are stories about the covenant between God and people. We hear of the struggle to keep that covenant, and of the many times people failed in living up to that covenant. But, even more so, we hear of a God, who, in spite of people's many failures, never abandoned the covenant made and remained faithful even in the face of rejection. And that rejection becomes most real in the dead body of Jesus on the cross.

God favors Noah and his sons as God establishes a covenant with all people. One important element about the Old Testament covenant is that God, not people, initiates the covenant. It is God who re-establishes the covenant over and over throughout history when people violate it. The examples of this are numerous: the fall of Adam and Eve; the killing of Abel; the disobedience in Noah's day; the tower of Babel; the covenant with Abraham; the covenant with Moses; the covenant with the prophets during the exile in Babylon; and when the time was right—God sent Jesus to model all covenants and to reconcile us to God and to one another.

As in Noah's day, it took forty days to flood and cleanse the earth of evil—so Jesus spent forty days to prepare himself to preach the Good News. As in Noah's day, there is a flood of waters to destroy the evil on earth—so Jesus goes into the Judean desert and into the Jordan river to signify that it will be his life that will conquer death and evil—and that from now on water will be seen as the life-giving sign of this covenant, which is for us the bath of baptism.

The covenant that Noah and Israel made a long time ago lives on even today, in people who share the vision and faith found in the Bible, in people who are called Jews and Christians and Muslims, in people who did not reject God, but accepted the call.

Yes, Christians, you and me, we are also carrying on the covenant of God with people! And for the Christian, that covenant is made clear in the life and death of Jesus of Nazareth. We are called to live as he lived, to serve one another, to love without limits, to give of ourselves, even if it kills us. In return, we have God's promise of eternal life. This is the covenant we possess along with all Jews and Muslims.

There are three questions to meditate on:
1. Do you realize you are, by baptism, involved in a covenant with God?
2. What are you doing to live up to this covenant?
3. Do you also realize that covenant is not exclusive and is shared by Jews and Muslims?

A HUNDRED FLOWERS

Let a hundred flowers blossom,
earth and air enough for endless
tubers, seeds, and pink carnations;
stones are stones and stones they must be,
people soar aloft like godlings,
but let shamrocks and the clover
blossom forth a hundredfold!

Cornflowers blue as bits of
heaven, poppies glow like gashes
morning stars along the sluiceways
coaxing to be seen by someone;
growing rampant in the poplars
mistletoe entwines and nestles,
spray of kisses bittersweet.

On his thorny stalk the balding
squire is blooming and is grieving
and no butterfly will find him;
twigs from tree trunks radiating
ferns engraved on frozen panes shall
flutter, and a hundred paper
roses yet shall come to bloom.

Fragile, still with stems unbroken,
these entangled wild and blindly,
those in caverns or on dung heaps,
others pressed by ice or pages,
or on tombstones—let a hundred
very different independent
nameless flowers come to bloom!

In a woods of dreamy jungle
stony roots and wiredrawn cobwebs,

labyrinth of words all whirling
dwells a man, a spindly bungler,
lily of the field, his eyes grown
misty, nearly blind with looking
for a spot beside a spring.

22.
LENTEN MEDITATION I

Readings: Genesis 2:7-9; 3:1-7 Romans 5:12-19 Matthew 4:1-11

In his most recent and best selling book entitled *The Gifts of the Jews*, Thomas Cahill, who is the former director of religious publishing for Doubleday, has this to say:

> It is no accident, therefore, that the great revelations of God's own Name and of his Commandments occur in a mountainous desert, as far from civilization and its contents as possible, in a place as unlike the lush predictabilities and comforts of the Nile and the Euphrates as this earth of ours can offer. If God—the Real God, the One God—was to speak to human beings and if there was any possibility of their hearing him, it could happen only in a place stripped of all cultural reference points, where even nature (which was so imbued with contrary, god-inhabited forces) seemed absent. Only amid inhuman rock and dust could this fallible collection of human beings imagine becoming human in a new way. Only under a sun without pity, on a mountain devoid of life, could the living God break through the cultural filters that normally protect us from him (Pg. 161).

In the Gospel, Jesus, himself goes into the mountainous desert to encounter God. The desert is where it all begins—for Israel and for Jesus. The desert is where it all comes clear—for Israel and for Jesus. The Christian too must follow in the footsteps of Israel and Jesus. We too must enter the mountainous desert to begin any spiritual journey.

It is for this reason that the Church has set up the season of Lent—the season we spend in the barren desert and on the lonely mountain. The Church strips its sanctuaries, imposes ashes instead of sprinkling water, curtails its music, and clears the way for a desert climate. Lent is a journey in and through the desert. And when we emerge, we hope and pray that it will be as Jesus and Israel—newborn, new people, new life, new heaven, and new earth. The fear we have is the possibility of emerging like Adam and Eve—our same old self!

Forty days and forty nights—to do what?
To listen to every word that comes from the mouth of God!

Forty days and forty nights—to do what?
To pray and fast and grow and become!

Forty days and forty nights—to become what?
To become able to re-enter life with vigor, energy, and enthusiasm.

And so, we enter the desert once again. We enter as Christians and hope to become better Christians. We enter as "fallible human beings" hoping to become human in a new way. We come baptized, confirmed, some married, some ordained, all looking for bread and healing. We come with open hearts and minds, receptive to the unknown, yet willing.

The desert is quiet and empty—what is there here for us? The desert is barren and hot—what will it produce for us? The desert is vast and arid—what do I want from it?

The answers will come—if you are willing to pray, fast, and avoid temptations. The answers will come—if you are honest with yourself about yourself. The answers will come—if you remain faithful to what has called you here—to whatever it is you try to evade, yet, welcomes you across the threshold. The answers will come—you might not like them—but they will still come.

The desert—our Lenten home for forty days and forty nights!

AND YOU PURSUE ME

And you pursue me.
And I evaded you
as long as I could.

Who did not push me or pull me,
but welcomed me across the threshold.
Who did not tear apart my veil of anguish,
but lifted it.
Who, simply with your voice,
would softly seduce me, that I was willing.

And you pursue me.
And I evaded you
as long as I could.

Once bound to every rumor heard of you,
now, beyond all fear, at last I wait for you.

And you pursue me.
And I evaded you
as long as I could.

23.
LENTEN MEDITATION II

Readings: Genesis 22:1-2, 10-13, 15-18 Romans 8:31b-34 Mark 9:2-10

Lent is a time of preparation for Easter! For new life! And when one is in the process of "preparing," one prefers to be alone, away from the crowd, able to concentrate, evaluate, see, and plan. And there are two places where one usually goes to enter the process of "preparing"—THE DESERT and THE MOUNTAIN!

THE DESERT is a lonesome, vast, dry, and hot experience (like in a kitchen preparing a meal). THE MOUNTAIN is a secluded, pinnacle, cool, and airy experience (like on the top floor of a library preparing for a test). Both places are sacred space—space where we see things differently and new, where we gain insight, where there are no disturbances, except in our souls, and where there are no surprises, except in our hearts.

Jesus went into the desert to prepare for his ministry. Jesus goes to the mountain to continue his preparation.

These Gospel stories are what Carl Jung would call "archetypal." Every great person in history or prehistory entered the desert or climbed the mountain as a symbol of the change and stamina necessary for the process of preparation. Noah and his family went into the ark, a sort of paradoxical desert since it floated on water; a sort of paradoxical mountain since the ark landed on a mountain when the flood subsided. Moses encounters his call from the burning bush on the mountain called Horeb. Israel wanders in the desert forty years preparing to become a nation. Abraham prepares for his covenant with God by taking his son Isaac to the mountain called Moriah.

Again—Jesus does both! He goes into the desert and he goes up on a mountain. These two stories tell us about the two aspects of any kind of real preparation.

In the desert, Jesus is tested and tempted. On the mountain, Jesus is transfigured, changed.

The Jesus story teaches the Christian that anything worthwhile in life needs to be prepared for. And that when real preparation is done, success is not necessarily the outcome. Jesus does not prepare himself to be successful. He prepared himself, like Moses and Elijah, to be faithful and remain faithful, even in the face of failure. Jesus' trial in the desert prepared him for the trials of his mission. Jesus' transfiguration on the mountain prepared him for the inner transformation every human must go through to become a faithful person.

The desert is low. The mountain is high. They symbolize the ups and downs of any real endeavor in life. The desert and the mountain are opposite extremes. They symbolize the extremes of remaining faithful to one's purpose in life. The desert is horizontal. The mountain is vertical. When they come together in a life, they form a cross.

For Jesus, faithfulness led to the cross. For Jesus, faithfulness was his stamina to survive trials and his openness to change.

The desert is all about survival; the mountain is all about openness. Both of these aspects, Jesus prepared for. He did these well. They served him well—all because he prepared for them in the desert and on the mountain.

As we Christians prepare for Easter, we need to do the same—enter a desert and climb a mountain. Where is our desert going to be? Where is the mountain we will have to climb?

Start looking now...
For the reign of God is at hand!
The time of fulfillment is now!

Reform your life…
Change your heart…
Strengthen your spirit…
Transform your soul…
Be transfigured!

TURN YOUR HEART TO ME

You I sought by day,
thought: in light you live.
Break the darkness then.
Turn your heart to me.

Dead, without a trace,
yet not dead enough
to deserve the grave.
Stolen from your hand
while you glanced away,
with no thought for me.
Turn your heart to me.

Plant new heart in me.
Give my mouth a voice,
my shade a body.
Dead is deaf-and-dumb.
There nobody knows.
Name has been erased.
Turn your heart to me.

If you will not send
me a glimpse of you,
I want no one else,
laugh my mask to stone
flee into the dark,
turn to wilderness.
Turn your heart to me.

REV. ROBERT E. ALBRIGHT

Streaks of morning light,
tear the darkness then.
Turn my heart in me.

24.
LENTEN MEDITATION III

Readings: Jeremiah 31:31-34 Hebrews 5:7-9 John 12:20-33

The word "lent" is an old English word that means "spring." The spring of the year—when trees bud, when grass gets green, when flowers peek through the ground, when the days grow longer giving more time in the light, when the air becomes warm, when people appear more and more outdoors, and when we Christians prepare for Easter.

Like spring announces summer—Lent announces Easter.
Like spring looks forward to summer—Lent looks forward to Easter.
As spring is new life—so Lent too is a time for new life!

Throughout Lent in church, we listen to story upon story about covenants of new life between God and people. We hear of the covenants between Noah and God after the flood; between Abraham and God after the attempt on Isaac's life; between Moses and God after the infidelity of Israel in the desert; between Israel and God after the exile in Babylon; and, most importantly, between God and all people through the Son of People, Jesus Christ, the Son of God.

In each of these stories, there is a thrust of new life. But this new life could come only if the past could be forgiven and forgotten. In each story, that's exactly what happened. God, in God's mercy, forgave people and held out another chance to live.

Wouldn't it be great if someone would come up to you and say: "I'll not remember any of our past problems. Let's start all over again." Wouldn't it be even greater, if you could go up to someone and say, "Let's not consider the things gone by, but let's forgive and forget and begin anew."

Jeremiah presents this vision, exactly, of a world where people would not look back on their mistakes and sins, brooding over them, but looking ahead to a future when things will be different. Yahweh forgives the past sins of Israel, and in doing so gives her hope and points her toward the future that Jeremiah envisioned.

This is life—to start all over again when we have failed! This is spring—the beginning of new life!

If we are to be a people who proclaim new life, if we are an Easter people, then we must live the covenant we have made with God. We cannot go on as though it were winter—frozen, cold, unrelenting, always reminding ourselves of the worst, imprisoning ourselves and others, brooding, and unforgiving. Is the season of Lent some sheer ritual, or are we serious about starting over again? If we are willing to start over again, are we willing to allow others to do the same? Can we forgive all the harm that has been done to us? Why do we always view Lent as a time for us to be forgiven, for us to return to God? Why isn't it also a time for us to forgive?

> The days are coming, says the Lord,
> when I will make a new covenant
> with the house of Israel and the house of Judah…
> I will be their God and they shall be my people…
> I will forgive their evildoing
> and remember their sins no more.

This prophecy of Jeremiah will not be fulfilled until you and I live as though we were God for one another.

WHY STAND STARING?

> Why stand staring at what has happened?
> Don't get lost in things of the past.
> I, says he, will begin something new.
> It's beginning already,
> haven't you noticed?

25.
LUKE'S BEATITUDES

Reading: Luke 6:12-26

Let me picture for you the scene in the Gospel you just read. At the northern end of the Sea of Galilee are some small mountains that drop to a level stretch of land forming a beach at the edge of the water. It is here that Luke places the event we have called "The Beatitudes." Along this beach many disciples of Jesus and a large crowd waited for him to come down—faceless humanity, stoically standing, the rich, the poor, tired, confused, worn out, no longer knowing how to go on. Some in shabby clothes, some forsaken, some richly clad. But all waiting on the beach—waiting for someone, anyone, some good news, a password, a key, a liberating word.

Then a voice is heard—someone starts toward the water—singing a song—dreaming a dream—hoarsely outshouting the pounding breakers of boredom, of defeat, of drudgery, of toil. That voice cries out and *blesses* those who find life so hard to face, who look at life like a sea that must be crossed, who are tossed like a bottle on the waves. That voice cries out and *cautions* those who find life easy.

"Blest are you poor, you who hunger, you who weep, you who are hated, ostracized, and persecuted—you should rejoice!" "Woe to you rich, you who are filled, you who laugh, you who are treated well by others—you should be careful!"

The voice says, no one can say what life is—you can only experience it or miss it. The voice says, there is no recipe for how to live life—you just live it, sometimes not even knowing of what use it is.

But the voice does say: I am the Way, I am the Good Shepherd, I am the Bread of Life. This voice echoed in a man, Jesus of Nazareth, a man who lived life to the full, who gave himself for others, who risked going where no roads go, who, even at the water's edge in the face of death did not falter or give up. The Gospel says of him that he gave himself totally even to death on a cross.

That same Gospel calls us to persevere, to experience life in whatever way it comes to us, not to give up. Wherever people live this way, they live as Jesus lived, they give life to others, they pass life on (one to another). This is all we need to go on—no pathway, no key, no beautiful house, only a hand on my heart and a mouth upon mine, people giving to people, a person with whom to live, life in spite of death!

SONG OF EXODUS

No manna from heaven,
no cloud for a sign,
only a hand on my heart
and a mouth upon mine.

Wintertime, on the beach, in shabby coats
soggy shoes, ranged like dark pilings
branded with numbers, stoically standing
waiting on the beach, a winter day.

We look but do not see; there is no horizon.
A shadow flits nearby and lightly skims the water—
a seagull snatching fish out of the foam,
gliding along the rolling whitecaps.

There are many of us on the beach,
most of us tired and confused, worn out,
no longer knowing how to go on, cold and shelterless,
forsaken now the old land, the wasteland.

Rich and poor, equal now, equally beaten:
turtle and hare, the snake, the greyhound;

the race is over at the water's edge,
that sea which no one can leap over.

Go? who dares go? how do we go, if we go?
who on one leg? who dares jump in headfirst?
who will dive in and swim beneath the breakers?
who will be tossed like a bottle on the sea?

Where to go? go naked or with clothes on?
perhaps like white dark-headed seagulls,
to glide along the surging crest of rolling waters,
hoarsely outshouting the pounding breakers:

No manna from heaven,
no cloud for a sign,
only a hand on my heart
and a mouth upon mine.

Does anyone know the password or have a key?
or have any food? or a dream? a tender memory?
anyone still know that hymn "He is my shepherd"?
someone starts toward the water, starts the singing:

No manna from heaven,
no cloud for a sign,
only a hand on my heart
and a mouth upon mine.

Someone makes a start—perhaps a wolf or shepherd
or underbrush or oak or creeping vine;
a rosebush shakes itself and is but brambles
a youngster carries his father on his shoulders.
Ten or twenty go, or one or maybe thousands
as if a song, as if the other shore were real
and death had died and sea had fled
with stinging salty waters—they all go singing:

I need no pathway
I need no key
no beautiful house
no manna from heaven
no cloud for a sign
only a hand on my heart
and a face turned to me
and a mouth upon mine
and a harp and a flute
like a woman and man
and the day breaking peacefully
over our pilgrimage
here in the world.

No manna from heaven,
no cloud for a sign,
only a hand on my heart
and a mouth upon mine.

26.
MIRACLE

Readings: Leviticus 13:1-2, 44-46 I Corinthians 10:31-11:1
Mark 1:40-45

From the Book of Leviticus, we get a real picture of how the people in Old Testament times viewed the lepers of their day. Considered outcasts, they had to hide their faces, had to call themselves "unclean," and had to live apart from the community. In the Gospel of Mark, we get a picture of Jesus, breaking through all tradition, leaping over centuries of prejudices, and risking rejection by his own peers as he cures a man from leprosy. As a result of this incident, he himself had to go apart from the community since they kept coming at him from all sides.

The story of a *miracle*—always fascinating to us Gentiles who live in a scientific age—always boggling our minds—always making us wonder, "What did he really do?" The story goes on to say: Jesus entered the life of a man with leprosy. In that encounter with the man Jesus, the leper began to see himself—who he really was and what he could be to himself and others—and so he cried, "Make me beautiful." Jesus, moved with pity, said, "I'll make you beautiful," and the leper was unmasked and began to discover what joy there is in being free enough to know himself, that he could not contain his joy and began to proclaim the whole matter in public.

All of us, I'm sure, have the desire to know who we are. Philosophy, theology, psychology, and sociology have striven for centuries to try to answer that fearful question: "Who are we?" or "Who am I?" or "What is life all about?" No answer has yet to be found. Yet we do not give up searching or at least asking the question.

Often we find ourselves searching into the Gospel stories, into the life of Jesus for the answers to our questions. What comes through to us as we read those Gospel texts and their learned commentaries over and over? We see a man who loves people—he is always with people—he seeks them out—and they seek him out. He avoids no one—he's not particular—he belongs to everybody, is always free for whomever he runs into. He wins people over by the open-minded way he walks up to them and he lets himself be won over and disarmed, for example by the leper who asks to be cured.

But he shies away from publicity—never plays to "his public"—he goes apart, to hidden places, to be alone, to pray. He wears no masks—he avoids the masks people so often wear, the masks that cause us to pretend to feel or to believe something that we really do not believe or feel: Like the mask of prejudice that called lepers unclean and kept them apart from the community. Like the mask of righteousness that causes us to easily condemn other religions or homosexuals. Like the mask of insecurity that forces us to refuse women into our sanctuaries or even the priesthood. Like the mask of pride that calls one race superior to another. Like the mask of a good-looking face or body. He wears no masks—but in the story you just read, he is willing to unmask all who call on him. He sees himself in all people and asks that all people see themselves in him. He calls upon us to do this also—to respond to one another, to love each other, even our enemies.

And to *love* means to know another person in the very source of that person's being —to bid him return there, seeing how alienated he is from himself. To appeal to the vision that is dying in that person. To say: "You, brother." "You, sister." To respond to another and to look that person full in the face as though you were God. To be God for her. To be the voice of her conscience. To go beyond our pride, our insecurity, and prejudices. To take a risk. To say to someone, "I'll make you beautiful," And to know when we can do this, then, we will know who we are—then, we will experience a miracle—then, we will see the face of God.

MAKE ME BEAUTIFUL

O make me beautiful, lay my face bare!
If you unmask me, you shall find me
and find more faces than you know,
find eyes that grope in the darkness,
heart that is prey to fear of fear.
O make me beautiful, lay my face bare!

I'll make you beautiful, lay your face bare!
If I unmask you, I will find you
and make you understand yourself anew,
and you shall live, stark and unfathomed,
a prey to naught and no one.
I'll make you beautiful, lay your face bare!

27.
MARRIAGE

Readings: Genesis 2:18-24 Psalm 128 Hebrews 2:9-11 Mark 10:2-16

Genesis—an ideal—a story of people—a way of life!

The Gospel—an ideal—a story of people—a way of life!

The Church—an ideal—a story of people—a way of life!

Since its inception, the Church has always upheld and proclaimed the ideals of marriage and family life presented by the stories you have just read. The teachings of the Church and the Bible seem to leave little room for interpretation of these ideals and have always condemned anything contrary to them. The Church has always frowned upon broken marriages, separation, and divorce; the Church gave no hope to people who could no longer live together as man and wife. The laws of the Church have forbidden divorce in the past and at present only tolerate such a thing as a legal measure to protect a Catholic's rights in the secular world. The laws forbid remarriage and even forbid a Catholic to marry a divorced person.

Because the Church's teaching has so strongly emphasized its disapproval of divorce, many divorced Catholics assume they are forbidden to receive communion and other sacraments. This is not true. Such exclusion, however, does apply to those divorced Catholics who remarry. They are regarded as living in sin. In such cases, they are cut off from the community. If they really want to go to communion, they have to leave their friends and family and go to a church in another community, where people will not know them. Or, if they remain in their parish, they run the risk of gossip and embarrassment.

Concern for groups with a special identity or specific problems is often singled out in the Church's public prayers and in parish life, but traditionally there has been only silence for the divorced. Many have interpreted this as a stigma. They have felt "left out" since it seemed to them that everything in the Church was oriented to the normal family situation—the picture painted by Genesis and the Gospel stories.

The Church's mission is to serve all of humankind! Like her Lord and Savior, she cannot distinguish among classes and types of people. She must proclaim and live the truth: that Jesus came to free all men and women. Despite these ideals, for the most part, she has ignored the needs of the divorced and of the separated for support and guidance. As a result, these people are held captive by the laws of the Church and the consequent prejudice of her members.

We, ourselves, often contribute to this captivity by our own closed mindedness. Very often, blinded by our pride, we fail to recognize that people are more important than laws. We presuppose that to follow a Church law is following the Gospel. Is it possible that two individuals, who, at the outset of their marriage, are filled with dreams, love, and hopes for children and a happy future, can discover after some time that this future is unattainable with each other? That they are no longer one and they dream no more together? And if this is so, is it necessary that they continue to live together as man and wife till death?

Becoming separated or divorced is not an easy way out of marriage! It is often marked by many psychological difficulties such as fear and guilt. It results very often in loneliness or antimale or antifemale tendencies. Where children are involved, there is often a measure of neglect since the mother or father must work to support the family that remains. Keeping that "broken family" together is no easy job (for a divorced man or woman). The children who are products of a "broken home life" very often find it a difficult thing to comprehend and even more difficult to explain it to kids in the neighborhood, teachers in school, and their school chums. A child in the traditional Catholic school system of the past would suffer many moments of painful doubt, confusion, and pressure as his religion teacher or the parish priest talked of the beauties of marriage and family life and displayed a personal and "official" disapproval of divorce and "broken homes."

It seems inevitable then, that the Church must rethink its position on divorce and the remarriage of divorced persons. Why is it taught that "no sin is too big to be forgiven" and in the case of the divorced who remarry no forgiveness can be sought? How can the Church go on teaching that murder, napalming children, and "just wars" are passable offenses when the divorced are refused reconciliation? Why are wrong choices in education, in government, and in business accepted, and yet the choice of a wrong partner in marriage can never be an accepted possibility?

Although much has been accomplished in shortening the procedures for annulments, this is not enough. For at least thirty years now, theologians and canon lawyers have been urging the Church to rescind its rules against the second marriage of divorced Catholics. Several years back the Dutch bishops began admitting divorced people to remarriage and all other sacraments. In this country of ours, every year now for the past number of years the National Divorced Catholics Conference unanimously adopted a resolution calling on the United States bishops to welcome back into full membership in the Catholic Church all men and women who have been separated from it by divorce and remarriage. It is common in many places here in our own country for remarried divorced persons, after reaching an understanding with their priests, to receive the sacraments in good conscience. They do this in the conviction they are sinless in a stable second marriage after a hopeless first one. But this solution is only partially satisfying, since the second marriage cannot be blessed. Interested and concerned bishops have set up a ministry to the separated, widowed, or divorced persons in their dioceses (SWORD), hoping to alleviate the pain and misery of so many people previously alienated by this same Church.

There is still much to be done. Looking back into the Gospel, the words of Jesus on divorce glare at us—all of us—not just the separated or divorced. He tells us again, as he does so many times in the Gospel, that we are people seeking perfection—striving for happiness—always moving forward—and he holds out the ideal. He does not condemn us if we fall on our journey toward this ideal. He forgave over and over. He blessed and broke bread over and over. He spoke about the future over and over—the same future we behold in the Book of Genesis. For the story of creation, the story of Adam and Eve is not a story about the past—about how things were—but rather a story of the future—about how things ought to be. And if each of us lives as Jesus did, if we can forgive, if we can support and help those who fall, if we can hold out the ideal by the way we live, then the future will be that moment when God can look at creation and say, "It is good!"

OF FIRE AND IRON

From fire and iron, sour and salt,
as wide as light and old as time,
from all that is we all are built
and always anew are born.
To be iron in the fire,
to be the salt and sweet and sour;
to live life for everyone,
so each of us is born.

To be the water for the sea
a word for another, so to be;
no one can know how great or small
to be sought and known and lost.
To be land of dusk and dawn,
at once to be here and yet be gone;
to hold your hand in mine,
and never to be lost.

To be as old and wide as light,
and water, thirst, and eager lips;
to be all things, yet nothing be,
we go to one another.

How far yet, no one can know
through melting fire that burns and glows;
for living in love and grief
we join with one another.

28.
RESURRECTION

The Scripture of the New Testament carries within it many different Easter messages—many different ways of expressing the Easter mystery. The oldest is from Paul, who experiences the Lord Jesus, and through this encounter with the risen and exalted Lord, proclaims that all (Jew and Gentile) who believe in Jesus and carry out his mission in this world have a true and personal relationship with him. Next, in historical sequence, is Mark, who brings us face-to-face with the Easter mystery, pointing to the fact that it is our responsibility to believe or not believe that Jesus is the Messiah and Son of God. Then there is Matthew who completes the picture of our relationship to and faith in Jesus by showing that he is always with us, at work in all we are and do—Emmanuel, God with us. At almost the same time, but in another locale is Luke whose message is that Jesus is alive—so alive, that when we hear the word and break the bread, it is the Lord! Jesus takes the initiative. If we recognize that it is he, then he gives us a share in his mission to preach the forgiveness of sins. And lastly, there is John who not only unites believers with Jesus, but shows this union as a step toward fuller union with the Father. For John as well as Luke, this is accomplished through the outpouring of the Spirit, the Spirit of Jesus, the same Spirit bestowed by Jesus on his apostles, the same Spirit who was present "in the beginning," the same Spirit who lives and sustains the world and the Church today.

It all seems so complete. Yet, I suggest we have missed something. Do you know what that could be? Think! What about the Easter message of Jesus? Is there one? What is it?

We have to probe very deeply to find the Easter message of each writer in the New Testament. And what happens when we put it all together? When we do, we discover in all those pages the Easter message of Jesus—and it is this: *Dying without rising has no meaning*! This is what makes Paul exclaim, "If Christ has not been raised, then your faith is in vain" (I Cor. 15:17)!

Let us reflect for a few moments on this message, for I believe it is the Easter message for all times: *Dying without rising has no meaning*!

Two people in love usually enter into some kind of relationship. As long as their love is never tested, they can enjoy their relationship. For love should include joy, peace, happiness, unity, faith, trust, eternity. However a paradox it may be, it is at the point of crisis, of disagreement, of infidelity, of "falling apart at the seams," of "upsetting the applecart," of betrayal, of sorrow, of dying, that true love is really manifested. It is here at this low point, this depression, this death, that love is tested. It is at this moment when death will either conquer or lose its sting. It is precisely here where a love relationship simply dies or rises to new life.

If two people are really in love and do not conceive of themselves as simply shackled by their relationship, their crisis becomes the only bondage, and their love for each other will conquer and free them, even though the crisis remains. When there is no real love, the only alternative is a hopeless death, separation, divorce, a living lie, annihilation.

To speak of death in this way is no less real and no less final than physical death. In the more ancient writings of the Old Testament, we find Israel applying the word *death* to sickness, rejection, political enslavement, sin, depression, separation, or any crisis within the life of the nation and its people. For Israel, the reality of death was any experience of loss or absence of goodness and love. They applied the term *resurrection* to the return to life of a person who, through illness, had fallen keen on the hands of death, or of a nation fallen from grace, which, in its lamentable state, compares only to a corpse. In this way, the vocabulary of *resurrection* was gradually formed: "to bring back to life," "to call forth," "to raise up," "to awaken," from the sleep of *death*.

To live is to love, to believe, and to trust. It is love that is stronger than death, faith that makes us persevere, and hope that makes us immortal. Listen to Israel in Egypt, to the prophets in Babylon, to Paul in prison, to the Jews in concentration camps, to Christians in South America, to blacks in Africa, to your neighbors, to Jesus on the cross, to yourself.

Whatever lives experiences death, and there is no doubt that death is everywhere in the world, in the Church, in you and me. The world is racked with the stench of war. The Church is defeated by the loss of its members. Our families are wrought with the struggle for survival. And you and me?—well, we are the world, the Church, and our family. Shall we die or rise? Can we fathom the Easter message of Jesus: *Dying without rising has no meaning*? Do we choose annihilation or eternal life? Is it our choice? Is it up to us?

It has been my personal and pastoral ministry to help people to fully live and not die in vain. I believe in death, but not without resurrection. Whether in the Church or the world around us—work, school, family, neighborhood, etc.—I do not see plunging ourselves into disagreement and discord with authorities whose power exceeds their mercy, whose emotions and fears are greater than their feelings and intellect, whose prestige and security are greater than their faith, and whose actions deny that anyone can trust another human being. Living this way is not only death, but also sheer annihilation. This kind of confrontation would result in demise without any hope for a future or for resurrection.

Nor do I suggest we give up who we are and what we believe in. Despite our shortcomings, our limitedness, our wavering, we are alive. And this is a sign of love. And real love will not prevent us from death, but it will go on calling us forth, bringing us back to life, raising us up, waking us up from the sleep of death. There is an old saying: *Don't get stoned on the way to crucifixion*!

We must live, love, suffer, and wait. We must grow strong in our union with other people. We must make each other beautiful, dry each other's tears, touch and soothe each other's wounds, make each other clean, and keep an eye on each other. We must break through the barriers and closed doors that people create around themselves. We must break through our own unwillingness to be touched by others. We should not be afraid to show each other our wounds. If each one of us takes the initiative, the risk, in reaching out to another, then not only the other, but we too will come to recognize who we are. Each of us must be like him whose name we bear—a child of God, a friend, a light, a shepherd, one who does not look out for oneself and does not go to death in vain and fruitless. We must recognize ourselves as his body, his risen body, living on in the world. We must take bread and break it for each other, and share our life's blood. Then we will not fear dying, for he is with us—our bread, and we—each other's bread.

I hope you are not waiting for a dramatic ending to this sermon. Rather, may it be a beginning. As "in the beginning," we are always involved in the process of creation, liberation, reformation, rebirth, reshaping our lives over and over again. The sermon is ending. Every ending is followed by a new beginning. This is the Easter message of Jesus: *Dying without rising has no meaning.* This is life—and we hope also death. This is Easter. This is resurrection. This is spring. This is love. This is God. This is you. This is me. This is people. And perhaps we people live!

SONG ABOUT PEOPLE

The birds can never live as men and women live.
They shelter in the trees and find refuge in their song.
They sow no seed, but dream—and their future is but death.

We people cannot live as water flows along—
so rapid and so fleeting and never feeling thirst.
The water goes on flowing, but people are not so.

The walls are not so old as men and women are.
They crack with age, but sorrow is quite unknown to them.
We people have to labor, but bricks and stones do not.

We people do not fall as trees when they are old.
We have our sons and daughters a future human life.
The trees must fall and die, but perhaps we people live!

29.
EASTER

Readings: Acts 2:42-47 I Peter 1:3-9 John 20:19-31

The Easter story in chapter twenty of John is the fulfillment of three promises that Jesus made to his disciples on the night before he died in chapter fourteen of that same Gospel. At the Last Supper, Jesus promised his disciples that:

1) He was going away—yet they would see him again;
"In my Father's house there are many dwelling places. If there were not, would I have told you that I am going to prepare a place for you? And if I go and prepare a place for you, I will come back again and take you to myself, so that where I am you also may be" (14:2-3).

2) That he was going to send the Holy Spirit to them;
"I will ask the Father and he will give you another Advocate to be with you always, the Spirit of truth, which the world cannot accept, because it neither sees nor knows it. But you know it, because it remains with you, and will be in you" (14:16-17).

3) Finally, that he would leave them the gift of peace;
"Peace I leave with you; my peace I give to you. Not as the world gives do I give it to you. Do not let your hearts be troubled and afraid" (14:27).

And so it was promised—and so it happened! After Jesus had risen from the dead—he came to show himself to his disciples once again—he grants them "peace"—then he breathes on them the Holy Spirit.

Somehow, the resurrection accomplished these three things in his disciples: It made them conscious that he was alive again. It put them at peace. And it gave them his abiding presence in the Holy Spirit.

However, there was one little addition to all this that wasn't present in any of the promises made at the Last Supper. It was the command to forgive sins.

"If you forgive people's sins, they are forgiven them; if you hold them bound, they are held bound" (20:23).

Somehow, peace and the Holy Spirit are linked with the forgiveness of sins. The *Spirit* of Jesus is the Spirit of love—and that Spirit grants the power to forgive and be forgiven. The *peace* Jesus gives is the peace that comes with forgiveness, the peace that comes with being forgiven, and the ability to forgive.

At this moment in time, the Western Hemisphere is torn apart once again by many wars. And war is always the absence of peace, the absence of love, the absence of forgiveness. In fact—war is the opposite of all that Jesus promised his disciples, his Church.

We cannot remain silent about the Easter Message in the Gospel of John. It always has been and remains a message of peace, love, and forgiveness. There is no Easter anywhere without these three gifts of the Lord Jesus.

If there is no Easter in war-torn areas of our planet, then there is no Easter anywhere—built on the promises of Easter: peace, love, and forgiveness. Our brothers and sisters at war might celebrate Easter in their churches, but they won't experience that mystery in their lives.

We ended the last millennium in war and we began the new millennium the same way!

When will they ever learn!?
Where have all the flowers gone? Long time passing.
Gone to graveyards, everyone.
When will they ever learn!? (Peter, Paul & Mary)

In this homily, I am stating something you all already know only too well. The question becomes for each of us individually and all Christians together, what can I do? What can we do? For the moment, I have only three answers:

The first is abstract and remote. Each of us can pray. All of us can pray. Prayer is opening ourselves up to God's Holy Spirit. The Holy Spirit is the activity of God in this world. Perhaps, then, if you pray enough, God will send the Holy Spirit to guide you to some action.

The second answer I have is more concrete and immediate: Check with your church and charity services in your area and see if there is something tangible, practical, and charitable that you can do to help people in war-torn areas of the world—and then DO IT! If it means a sacrifice on your part, it even becomes a form of prayer.

My third answer is that we talk to one another about all of this. Let us seek solidarity with each other in faith. Dialogue about these life-threatening issues. Spend quality time with your friends and family conversing and expressing your concerns.

This planet is the most perfect and ideal planet we know of in this entire cosmos to produce, support, and develop life. What we humans are doing to it is shameful and almost unforgivable. Therefore, let us talk and dialogue, negotiate and learn, try to understand, and above all learn to forgive. And finally, let us pray:

SO NEAR YET SO FAR

Unseen yet present, everywhere active,
your word is near, you are there in the silence,
people admit you, seeking and finding you.

People of flesh, of light and of earth rock,
firm, yet of blood, surging like the flood waters
these are your people, your city here on earth.

Earth is as we are, all that we make it.

Breathe us wide open, to make us your new earth
and your new heaven, being your peace on earth.

30.
DEATH AND LIFE AFTER DEATH

The spirituality of the first century in the Church was to give one's life for the Gospel. Martyrdom, then, was common. Of the one hundred and seventy-three saints named in the present church calendar, forty-nine are martyrs. From its inception, Christianity was a religion that never professed the fear of death, but welcomed it. Like their model, Jesus Christ, Christians are called upon to confront death, believing that they too, like him, would rise someday from death and live happily ever after with God in heaven. The prayer of the Church has been for centuries: "If you have saved your son from death, O God, if he, dead and buried, lives on with you: then, likewise, save us."

Long after martyrdom became unfashionable, Christians adopted a new mode of living the Gospel, but employing the same theology. They began dying to the world—going off into caves, hermitages, and monasteries where they lived as though they were dead. They gave up all rights to worldly possessions—poverty. They gave up the right to marriage and reproduction—celibacy. They gave up the right to live according to their own will—obedience. In a sense, this was a new kind of martyrdom, a new way of dying. It was called, "dying to self," or as we have termed it today, "self-denial."

For centuries, this spirituality pervaded the Christian world. Liturgical seasons such as Lent, pious practices such as fasting and abstinence, religious discipline such as scourging oneself or wearing a hair shirt, the development of a new sacrament called "penance"—all of these brought the spirituality of the monasteries into the everyday life of the laity. Perhaps you were raised on it. Remember how much easier it felt to be dead than to get up for daily Mass in grammar school? Remember Fridays when you couldn't eat meat or when you got to be twenty-one and had to fast every day during Lent? That was a taste of death. Dying to self was the Church's intention. Death was and still is the focus of Christianity. A Christian is someone who does not fear death, but lives it every day so that when that final moment comes, he or she is able to face it with joy and acceptance.

Over the past twenty centuries, Christian theologians (having nothing else to do) began speculating about the afterlife—what goes on beyond death. Scripturally they realized that the good would be rewarded (heaven) and the wicked would be punished (hell). But how about those in between—those who die imperfect enough not to go to heaven and not that bad that they should go to hell? Easy enough! *Purgatory*—a place to burn away the imperfections before eventually going to heaven. And how about unbelievers? They obviously would be damned forever. As infant baptism became common, so did questions about those who were not baptized. Did they see God after death? Certainly not! That would be unfair. So let's send them to...to...*Limbo*!

For the Christian, then, life after death is determined by life before death. This theology has not changed in two thousand years, but today we interpret it in different terminology. The terminology of the past is giving way to a new vocabulary about death, even though the theology is basically the same. We do not live in such an analytical society as our ancestors, and therefore, our ideas today are more personal, more human, and so is our terminology. No one today wishes to categorize the dead into such distant and impersonal terms as *purgatory* or *limbo*. Also, we are beginning to see that our theology of the past (with its emphasis on martyrdom) failed to see deeper into the New Testament passages, which would allow another view of death. As we attempt this today, we are discovering a whole new philosophy of living (not just of dying) set forth in these same New Testament pages. This new awareness, this discovery of a balanced view of life and death, is leading modern Christian theologians to form a new consensus about death and perhaps even a new theology of death.

I can best summarize this new theology on death by the following statement: only at death can a person take the stance by which he or she will definitely win or lose his or her salvation. Since about 1932, this statement has been increasingly taken to mean that that moment (the moment of death) brings the only free, self-determination of human life.

Let me explain. Death has traditionally been defined by Christian philosophy and theology as the separation of body and soul. Analyzing this classic definition of death, the famous German theologian, Father Karl Rahner, concludes that it is important, but inadequate. The importance of this definition is the understanding that life goes on after death. The inadequacy of this definition is its failure to speak of death as a personal and totally human event. Death cannot be merely an irruption from without (caused by a storm or a flood, a car accident, old age, cancer, a shot in the heart, or a blow to the tree trunk); it must also be an act that one personally performs. In the view of Rahner, then, death is an activity brought about by the person him or herself—a maturing self-realization that embodies what a person has made of him or herself during life.

Just as the song sings, "death is in our blood," so the new theology of death is formulated. But we can see that it is no different than the theology proclaimed by St. Paul in his letters. In both theologies, then, (the new and the Pauline) death is present in every act of human existence as its own end, something not yet possessed, but proper to every being. Paul says, "I face death every day" (I Cor. 15:31).

Let's create a picture of what theologians are saying about death today: An unborn child is given an existence it did not request. A newborn child receives a heritage and environment it could not choose; parents, race, time, and place of birth it did not select. Childhood and adolescence is a time of being dragged through currents of family, circumstances, culture, society, education, and religion one does not have any say in. Soon, however, the conscious self awakens and rises high above the currents. Born into a community whose structure was imposed upon her, a person gradually becomes aware of her personal autonomy. Her actions become increasingly independent; the environment that once held her widens; her self-consciousness deepens. She becomes involved and begins to grow. She moves from community to communion. Then, in old age, activity dwindles; the environment narrows, consciousness and freedom seem to diminish. The weakening body can no longer support further growth and communion. Like the womb, our mother's lap, home, family, school, the physical body too gives way to something new. The human person grows by tearing herself away from previous environments that have become like so many prisons. As the infant must leave the womb to carry out its own biological functions, so also we must someday leave this body if we are to carry out fully our own proper activity. This is the act we call death.

Therefore, there is an activity in death on the part of the person dying. It is an act of personal self-fulfillment, an act we perform from inside us. Death, then, becomes a transformation and a final option. It is our opportunity for posing our first completely personal and totally free act (with no strings attached). Another modern theologian, Ladislaus Boros, would state here that this would be the most opportune moment to encounter God and for a final decision about eternal destiny. For the modern Christian, then, as for St. Paul (one of the greatest Christians in our history), death is the moment he encounters Christ personally and with the total free power of his being chooses either to reject Christ or to establish a personal and definite relationship with him.

Now we can return to some of our age-old problems. For example, how about the salvation of the unbeliever? When we view death as the final option, this old problem is placed in a new perspective. The unbeliever is able to choose salvation in the very act of choosing death. The ancient question of infant salvation also finds a new solution. In the hypothesis of death as a final option, the infant would have the opportunity for a fully mature decision at the instant of death. Therefore, while countless children may leave us during infancy, no one dies an infant. Thus we might eradicate the words *limbo* and *purgatory* from our theology. When death is seen as perfect self-fulfillment, a free and complete act, final option, encounter with God, then purgatory would be instantaneous, the very passage that we effect in our final decision. And how long have we heard it said that at the moment of death your whole life passes before you?

Let's clear up at least one of the many confusions that might be occurring in your mind. Even though death is the first truly, completely free act we ever make in our lifetime, it is still our final act. Death is both first and last, alpha and omega, the beginning and the end, the point toward and from which eternity is born, the one thing that gives meaning to all that goes before and all that follows. And that leads us to our final point in this sermon—a question that haunts us!

Why is there, in Christian theology, such an insistence on the importance of the death of Jesus? But with that question comes another sub-question: Why couldn't any moral act have been the adequate expression of Christ's redeeming obedience? Well, if we remember what has been said about our Christian theology of death so far, a possible answer emerges not only for the Jesus question, but for our own deaths as well. The developing human reality of Jesus (who he is) reaches its perfection in his death. It was only at this moment (in this first and final act) that he was able to give the fullest human expression to who he was and what he had done with his life. In other words, we have a new twist to an old theology. The way you live life doesn't necessarily have anything to do with the afterlife. But the way you die definitely gives meaning to life before and after death. Perhaps this is the context in which Mark makes this comment about the death of Jesus: "When the centurion who stood facing him saw how he breathed his last he said, 'Truly this man was the Son of God'" (Mark 15:39)!

We have returned to our old theology of death with more insight, because of a new theology. We have asked again (as is the Christian quest): Does death have any meaning? The answer to this question (as you can see now) will be different for everyone reading this sermon. Because you will give the answer, personally and freely, the moment you choose to die.

For the Christian, then, life gives meaning to death and death gives meaning to life. Living and dying give meaning to each other, but it is only **people** who can give meaning to both.

YOU WHO KNOW

You who know what goes on in people,

119

the hoping, doubting,
dullness, passion, pleasure, wavering

You who discern our thoughts
and measure all our words by truth
and grasp at once the things
we cannot put in words

You try our hearts
and you are greater than our hearts,
you keep an eye on every one of us

and no one ever lacks a name with you
and no one falls without falling in your hands
and no one lives without living toward you.

Still, no one ever saw your face,
you are inaudible.
In all this world your voice never echoes,
deep in the earth nor from the heights of heaven.

And no one who has entered death's domain
ever returned
to bring us back your greetings.
With tender ties to you, we bear your name.
You alone know what that means,
not we.

With eyes unopened we journey through the world.
Yet sometimes we ourselves recall a name,
an ancient story we were handed down,
touching a man who trembled with your power,
Jesus of Nazareth, a Jewish man.

In him your grace was said to be transparent
your gentle, constant ways,
and we were told,

there came to light in him for good
what you are really like:
defenseless, selfless servant of people.

He was the way we all would want to be:
a child of God, a friend,
a light, a shepherd,
one who did not live to look out for himself
and did not go to death in vain and fruitless.

One who on his final night
among the living
took the bread and passed it all around,
and spoke the words:
take, eat, this is my body—
thus should you do to keep my memory.

Then raising high the cup, he spoke the words:
this is the new covenant, this is my blood,
and I shall shed it
that your sins may be forgiven.
Whenever you shall drink this cup,
think then of me.

To keep his memory
therefore, now we take
this bread; and break it
for each other,
that we may realize
what lies ahead for us
if we should choose
to follow after.

If you have saved
your son from death,
O God, if he
dead and buried

lives on with you:
then, likewise, save us
keep us alive
pull us, as well
through our dying
now.
And make us new,
for why save him
and not save us?
Aren't we
every bit as human?

ABOUT THE AUTHOR

Rev. Robert E. Albright is a retired Catholic Priest of the Archdiocese of Baltimore. He has served as the Catholic Campus Minister at Towson University for the twenty-six years prior to his retirement in July 2006. Previous to this, Father Bob served as campus minister at the University of Maryland Baltimore County for two years and then at Goucher College for three years. During all these years, he served first as acting director and then as director of Ministry to Higher Education for the Archdiocese of Baltimore. His other ministerial work includes nine years in two parishes as associate pastor and eight years teaching religion, music, German and English in elementary and secondary schools. Prior to his thirty-seven years as a priest, he was a member of the Brothers of the Christian Schools for thirteen years.

He received his undergraduate degree in Education and Modern Languages from LaSalle University in Philadelphia, where he also pursued graduate studies in Liturgical Music and Theology. He continued graduate studies at Catholic University in Washington, D.C., and Loyola College and St. Mary's Seminary in Baltimore.

Through teaching a scholarly approach to the Bible over the past forty-five years, Father Bob has explored greater interfaith issues at the Institute for Christian and Jewish Studies of Baltimore. His studies led him to the Catholic Center for Holocaust Studies at Seton Hill University in Greensburg, Pennsylvania, through which he traveled to Israel twice to study at the International Center for Holocaust Studies at Yad Vashem in Jerusalem. Father Bob has been to Israel over twelve times leading Study Tours And Retreats (**STAR**), as well as doing private research in Biblical sites and studying the Palestinian/Israeli situation.

At the moment, Father Bob is engaged in numerous interfaith activities, as well as publishing seven volumes of his sermons and homilies. He also belongs to numerous associations and organizations that support his work and accomplishments. In 2006, he was the recipient of the Annual Greenblatt Award, given by the Baltimore Jewish community to persons who do outstanding work in Holocaust education and programs.

His other areas of interest and study include male spirituality, creation spirituality, ecological spirituality, liturgical music, Christology, ecclesiology, drama, public speaking, teaching, preaching, and Western liturgical traditions, especially the sacramentology of the Roman Catholic Church.

3319441

Made in the USA